"The true and lasting story  how you deal with the pain, lo 1a of any source—is what matt /ides you with a pathway to de ɔain. It's the real deal that puts y .ce to turn your tragedy into triumph."

—Dave Roever
President and CEO
Operation Warrior Reconnect of Roever Foundation

"*Life Beyond the Scars* is, at its core, a gift to all of us. While Charity's retelling of her physical journey is riveting, it is her amazing detail of her mental, emotional, and spiritual struggles and growth that will keep you from putting this book down until you are done. I consistently found myself saying throughout the book, "I've felt the same way!" as she shared her thoughts and questions about purpose, adversity, and contentment in life.

You won't be the same after reading this book. Each day will become a new opportunity to live, love, and see others in ways you never thought possible. The callout quotes she shares throughout the book will become your guides to making more life-giving choices every day. *Life Beyond the Scars* is a must-read for anyone seeking to find clarity in their life and seeking to trust God more when facing difficulties of any kind."

—Jones Loflin
Co-author, *Juggling Elephants*

"If you'd like to mature in your faith, read this book. If you need a silver-linings-and-glasses-half-full kind of life, Charity can teach you what you need to know and do. She beautifully tells her compelling story, accurately uses relevant scriptures, and humbly explains what she learned from her injuries and recovery. You will benefit! I want to know the God of the Bible like she knows Him. You will, too! He is our real hope!"
—Dr. Kathy Koch, Founder of Celebrate Kids
Author of *Five to Thrive, Start with the Heart,*
Screens and Teens, and *8 Great Smarts*

LIFE BEYOND THE SCARS

FINDING HOPE IN TRAGEDY

CHARITY FREELAND

Photo Credit: Anne Gibbins, Carl Freeland, Shriners Children's Texas

Library of Congress Control Number: 2021914716

Paperback: 978-1-64746-864-4
Hardback: 978-1-64746-865-1
Ebook: 978-1-64746-866-8

Dedication

Mama, you planted the seed of faith in our lives. Faith was your greatest gift. You lived a life of loving out loud, right in front of us. Your words, your strength, and your courage have tethered us in the worst of storms, permanently anchoring us to Jesus. You've been our biggest fan and our most vigorous champion. I'm so grateful that you're experiencing the fullness of joy and can watch over all of us from your heavenly home. We miss you every day.

CONTENTS

Foreword ix

Prologue xi

Introduction xiii

PART 1: SURVIVING

Chapter 1: The Accident 3

Chapter 2: Choices 19

Chapter 3: Healing 43

Chapter 4: Grieving Losses 65

Chapter 5: Faith 79

PART 2: OVERCOMING

Chapter 6: Scars 97

Chapter 7: Victim Versus Overcomer. 111

Chapter 8: Facing Fears. 127

Chapter 9: Lies and Truths 147

Chapter 10: Acceptance. 165

PART 3: BEYOND THRIVING

Chapter 11: The Work of Suffering 187

Chapter 12: What is it to Thrive?. 195

Chapter 13: Hope and Wholeness 211

Epilogue 223

Final Note from Charity 225

Chapter Discussion Questions. 227

Acknowledgments 235

About the Author 237

FOREWORD

I've known Charity Freeland for nearly two decades. Our friendship is far beyond casual. It is far beyond an emotional connection or a relationship based on proximity or common interests. It is spiritual.

Our friendship found its footing through mutual experiences in pain. We both have the challenge of rising above the scars that have left their mark for all to see, although our suffering stems from totally different origins. Charity's tragic injury was the result of an automobile accident and mine of war. Though the sources are not alike, the pain and suffering are similar.

Another difference is that I found solace in purpose and passion. Charity could not. What glory is there in an automobile accident? What purpose and passion are born from a car wreck? Charity discovered, however, that the origin of tragedy is not of value. The source can be war, self-sacrifice for a cause, or an accident; the unhinged pain is the same.

The true and lasting story of Charity's experience is that how you deal with the pain, loss, and suffering—from trauma of any source—is what matters.

Charity and I share the reality of disfigurement and loss of identity; however, we have not lost hope. Charity faced even more than I can comprehend. A woman's beauty is her identity. Even though amazing surgery has offered partial restoration, doctors can never fully restore Charity's natural, physical beauty. Even so, she radiates a beauty so rich, it leaves you with a sense of knowing she is changed but not broken. The following pages reflect the awesome character of the One who brought about beauty from ashes, praise from pain, and wisdom from suffering.

Pay attention to the incredible lessons learned from suffering and shared from the heart of a warrior. *Life Beyond the Scars* provides you with a pathway to deal with disappointment and pain from any source that might seek to destroy you. Charity shares the principles of recovery that apply to any of life's challenges. Seek out her wisdom in this gripping story of victory. This *ain't* book learnin', my friend. It's the real deal that puts you in the driver's seat of choice to turn your tragedy into triumph. Take control of your life as Charity did. Do not let anything deny you your destiny.

My respect for this woman is unlimited. In my own words, "You go, girl!"

Dave Roever
President and CEO, Operation Warrior Reconnect
of Roever Foundation

PROLOGUE

By Roseanna Freeland Roberie

I have learned that each of us experiences earthquakes—circumstances that rock our individual worlds. Some we don't even feel. Others reveal themselves as slight tremors. At times, they fracture the foundations of who we believe ourselves to be. An experience might break us completely, revealing an insurmountable abyss between us and our goal. Then, some of these earthquakes completely shatter everything, leaving us no choice but to pick up the pieces and rebuild.

Logically, I've still not reconciled the inequality of these earth-shaking events or how or why some people face more numerous or arduous trials than others. I've spent years sulking at the unfairness of it all. It wasn't until about four or five years after the accident that I had a conversation with Charity. I was sobbing, reveling in guilt that she was still enduring the pain of an accident. I would give anything for it never to have happened. She took my face in her hands and told me we couldn't think that way; she liked the person she was today much more than the person she had been before.

Today I know it is in the aftermath of our earthquakes, especially those that shatter our worlds, that opportunities always lie before us. In these moments, we have the most profound choices to make, decisions that forever affect our lives' trajectories. It is amid our most significant adversity that we learn who we truly are. If we look closely, we can see the facets of God's design in our characters by simply focusing on His goodness in the middle of it all.

Words will never adequately describe how honored I am and how in awe I remain about the depth of God's love for me and the kindness he bestowed on me when he chose me to be the first little sister of Charity Freeland. To know her is to love her. And if you look closely, you can see what you feel when you are around her—the warmth and care of God's love shining through her in everything she does.

Our lives changed the night of the accident forever, but now, twenty-seven years later, I am ever so thankful for the impact it made on our eternity.

INTRODUCTION

*Now to Him who is able to do far more abundantly **beyond** all that we ask or think, according to the power that works within us.* (Ephesians 3:20 NASB, emphasis added)

I don't want this book to be about physically surviving burns. Honestly, there are plenty of good books out there that share the ins and outs of burn treatment, just as there are books about overcoming incredible trauma. I wanted the focus of my book to be different.

The focus of *Life Beyond the Scars* is my ongoing journey toward wholeness. I believe feeling whole or complete is what most of us want. Or at least I do.

I want to:

- know God for who He is.

- live from the knowledge that God is good.

- trust Him with all of me.

- see myself and others the way He sees us.

- rest secure in who God created me to be.

- receive every single thing He has for me.

- be content with what God has provided me.

- pursue my life knowing I'm unconditionally loved; I have incredible value and a purpose.

- love others well.

- live without fear, insecurity, jealousy, anger, or strife.

- have joy and peace to mark my days.

- be grateful.

- know I'm fulfilling my purpose.

- matter.

All these things are attainable here on Earth. I have tasted them, and I want more. That's why I say it's an ongoing journey toward wholeness. From my perspective, wholeness goes beyond surviving, overcoming or even thriving. Wholeness represents freedom, living in truth, living loved, and living to love. It is who I am when Christ lives in me and I in Him.

Before I begin sharing the lessons I've learned on my journey, I want to share some facts—okay, maybe several points.

I don't want this whole book to be about injuries resulting from an accident more than twenty-five years ago. The truth is I have learned many lessons from my accident, the resulting burns, hospital stays, treatments, therapy sessions, scars, and surgeries. The accident changed me; it altered the course of my life and opened my eyes to my purpose.

My injury exposed things I believed about myself from a very early age and forced me to confront some harsh truths. One of these truths was that I felt that *others* who were disabled or not "picture perfect" had value, purpose, and beauty. They were worthy of being fully loved. But I could not see *myself* that way. Honestly, I couldn't see myself that way *before* my accident. My scars forced me to confront the self-hatred that fueled my perfectionism—a standard that was no longer achievable (as if it ever were). In many ways, this single realization began my journey toward wholeness.

Upon meeting me, most people wonder what happened; that is normal human curiosity. If you are wondering the same thing, you're in luck. We're going to get that out of the way right up front. I share this part of my story, not so you will feel sorry for me or start comparing your pain to mine, but so you have all the facts.

MY SCARS FORCED ME TO CONFRONT THE SELF-HATRED THAT FUELED MY PERFECTIONISM

Each of us has our own "worst pain." Whatever that distress is for you, it is valid. It needs healing, regardless of the degree or visibility. Likewise, no matter how much you or I have suffered, others have endured much more loss, trauma, or abuse. But here's a lesson to keep in mind: Life is not a competition; it's a journey—to wholeness.

PART I

SURVIVING

1

THE ACCIDENT

"Mama, can I borrow the car tonight? Roseanna wants to go with her friends to the Mardi Gras dance at the high school. I thought Don and I could chauffeur—take them wherever they want to eat and for their pictures. Then we'll take them to the dance, pick them up after, and have them home by eleven."

Roseanna and I were sisters and good friends. Since I was two years older and could drive, I often took her friends and her places on the weekends. Even though I was a senior, and

Roseanna was a sophomore, she was more popular than me, and I liked that I could be a part of her life.

"I guess so," Mama replied, "but I thought Mr. Jimmy was going to run them around."

"Well, this way, he doesn't have to, and I would really like to do it."

Zanna (our family's nickname for Roseanna) and I got dressed for the dance. I put on my nice jeans and a short-sleeved, dressy blouse. I freshened up my makeup and checked the mirror. Pleased with how I looked, Roseanna and I were ready to go.

It had been raining since late afternoon, which was not unusual in Houma, Louisiana.

"Charity, Mr. Jimmy called and offered to drive. Why don't you let him?" Mama asked, sounding uneasy.

"Don't worry, Mama. I'm already dressed, and I'm happy to go."

I called Don. "We're just about to leave. I'm going to pick up Nikki first, and then I'll come get you before we get James and Scotty."

"Okay, babe. See ya soon."

It was already dark outside when we climbed into the 1966 Ford Falcon. It had a bench seat in front, which was one reason Papa bought it; the whole family could fit. The other reason was its age. He enjoyed working on old cars.

When we picked up Nikki, Roseanna scooted to the middle of the seat, and Nikki slid in beside her. None of us buckled up.

"Roseanna, do you have any money for tonight?" I asked as I drove to pick up Don.

"No, I forgot to ask Mom," she responded.

"I'll just run by the ATM at Rouses and grab some cash then."

We turned onto Martin Luther King Boulevard, a four-lane major road on the edge of town. We pulled into the parking lot at the grocery store, and I ran in to get cash.

On the way back to the car, I recalled a conversation from work earlier that day. I had been visiting with two friends, Beth and Tammy, on my break. Beth was a Christian lady in her thirties. Tammy was a few years older than me; she was married with two children and had one on the way. I don't remember exactly how our conversation moved from babies to seatbelts, but I do remember stating matter-of-factly, "I don't wear my seatbelt."

"Seatbelts save lives. Do you know how many serious injuries happen because people don't wear their seatbelts?" Beth asked. "Anyway, it's the law. As Christians, we're to obey the laws of the land. It doesn't hurt to wear it, just in case."

"Papa never wears his. He says it's not illegal since we drive an old car that didn't originally have any. They were installed afterward," I explained.

Break time was over, and that's all Beth said.

As I avoided puddles on the way back to the car, our conversation replayed in my mind. I didn't want to disobey God, so I put on my seatbelt when I got back in the car. Being an older car, it had a lap belt like those on airplanes. You flipped one side up to release it.

Back on the road, I accelerated to the posted fifty mph speed limit as we chatted and sang along to the radio—"Hero" by Mariah Carey.

Suddenly, the steering wheel jerked to the left. It scared me as I had never felt the car do this before. If we went much further left, we would be facing oncoming traffic. I slammed on the brakes, causing the vehicle to hydroplane. We spun around 180 degrees on the wet road.

"We're going to wreck!" I yelled as I felt the car sliding backward on the wet road into oncoming traffic.

A car struck us from behind, and the gas tank exploded when another vehicle smashed into the one that had hit us. Finally, we came to a stop, and I grabbed my door handle, wrenched it, and pushed the door open.

"I can't open my door! I can't open my door!" Nikki yelled.

The car had landed at an angle in the ditch. With the door against the ground, Nikki couldn't get out on the passenger side. Flames engulfed the cabin of the vehicle. Roseanna climbed over the seat and out the broken back window, then she helped Nikki out the same way. She thought I was right behind her.

I tried to step out of the driver's door, but my seatbelt restrained me.

The tires exploded one by one. Roseanna stood several yards away, still expecting me to emerge from the car. When she saw I wasn't coming, she lurched forward to get me.

It was a three-car accident on a busy road early in the evening, witnessed by a state trooper driving in front of us. Upon seeing the event unfold in his rear-view mirror, he flipped around, called emergency services, and was one of the first people on the scene. He approached the car and saw Roseanna and Nikki climb out. He saw Roseanna head back toward the car for me, caught hold of her, and held her back. "There's nobody in there," he insisted.

"My sister's in there!" She screamed.

He held Roseanna in a bear hug to keep her from running into danger while trying to convince her to get into the arriving ambulance.

"I can't get out!" I shouted.

"You *have* to get out!" Roseanna yelled at me.

Zanna looked back expectantly at the trooper holding her, hoping he had heard my words and would do something. He hadn't and didn't.

Onlookers tried to help, but they had to back up because of the heat. One of the ambulances arrived, with two others on their way. Flames surrounded me as I struggled to undo my seatbelt. I fumbled and pulled at the latch, but it wouldn't disconnect. With fire all around me, I didn't feel pain. I was on fire, but I didn't feel anything except the determination to get out of there. Fast.

The problem was, I couldn't see the seatbelt clasp clearly through the flames. My efforts to free myself were proving futile.

I realized I couldn't get out on my own. I yelled, "Somebody's gotta cut it!"

Within seconds of the words escaping my mouth, the seat belt miraculously snapped. I've always believed an unseen angel came and cut my seatbelt—with a giant sword, of course.

The door had re-latched when I tried to exit the car. I pulled the handle, shoved the door open, and climbed out.

"*Stop! Drop! And roll!*" Somehow the words from my kindergarten safety lessons came to me as I rolled out of the car on fire.

Once Roseanna saw I was out of the car, she collapsed. Emergency workers carried her to the waiting ambulance.

A stranger used his jacket to put out the flames burning my clothing. He stepped away as the ambulance workers surrounded me.

I heard someone say, "Go get a body bag."

Thankfully, there had been a couple of off-duty EMTs walking out of the store next door just as the accident happened. They immediately ran to the scene to help. One was standing nearby, ready to assist, and saw me move. He alerted the others, and suddenly everyone jumped into action. Someone cut off my jeans. Someone else cut off my class ring and the treasured watch Don had given me for Christmas.

While they worked, the ambulance workers asked me questions.

"What is your name?"

"How old are you?"

"Where were you going?"

"Was there anyone else in the car?"

I answered all of their questions and asked about my sister and Nikki. Miraculously, Nikki was okay. They told me my sister was going in the ambulance and would be alright. As soon as another rescue vehicle arrived, the techs loaded me into the back. They must have given me medication as we drove because I don't remember the ride to the hospital.

What felt like a flash and a blur had taken almost an hour. Worried, Don called my parents, informing them I hadn't arrived. He had been standing outside his house, waiting for me, when he saw flames across the field.

My parents quickly got into my dad's old 1967 Ford Pickup and went to look for us.

Our younger sister, Christina (Christy), stayed home with our two-year-old brother, Clay. She answered the phone when the hospital called to report that Roseanna was in an accident and had been admitted.

"My other sister, Charity, was in the car too. Is she there? Is she okay?" Christy asked.

The employee answered, "All I can tell you is that Roseanna is here."

The hospital called back once more, looking for our parents. By that time, Christy was acutely distressed. She begged them for information about me, but they couldn't tell her anything. She concluded if they wouldn't say anything about me, I must be dead.

When my parents checked in with her, all she could choke out was, "Mama, go to the hospital."

Sounding tired and resigned, Mama simply responded, "Okay, baby, I love you."

By the time they got to the hospital, Don was already there. He was frustrated because security wouldn't let him see me. I don't think they let anyone in because I was in such bad shape.

The hospital staff surrounded me and asked the same questions the ambulance workers had.

The doctors seemed perplexed about what to do with me. My injury was too severe to be treated in their hospital, and the terrible weather prevented them from immediately transferring me to the nearest burn hospital located in Baton Rouge. Knowing that the chances of my survival were slim, they used their knowledge and made the most of their limited facilities to keep me alive over the next few hours.

As the effects of the burns started to register in my brain, my body convulsed and went into shock. I tried to hold back my cries, but the pain was obvious. The medical staff administered more medication, and temporary relief washed over me. I slept some, but any time the doctors or staff moved me, searing pain woke me and made my body shake uncontrollably. Medication delivered through an IV helped take the edge off the incredible pain.

Later I learned that I only had a 1 percent chance of living through the first night. I had sustained burns over 75 percent of my body, and Roseanna's burns covered 30 percent of her body.

> I ONLY HAD A ONE PERCENT CHANCE OF LIVING THROUGH THE NIGHT.

Meanwhile, back home, Christy was taking care of Clay. She had taken the calls from the hospital looking for our parents and feared the worst. Caring for two-year-old Clay tethered her emotionally and physically while she waited for help or news to arrive.

While waiting for the weather to clear, Papa went home to check on Christy and Clay. Christy told me later that he looked more exhausted than she had ever seen him. Papa pulled her close on the couch beside him, and they cried together as he filled her in on what had happened. Soon, they received the news that there was enough visibility to get us on a helicopter and send us to the burn hospital. Papa picked up Mom from the hospital, and they raced to Baton Rouge.

THE HOSPITAL

I woke up in a strange room with my parents by my side. They had been waiting for hours for me to wake up. I couldn't move, and my vision was blurry. I tried to speak, but the words wouldn't come out.

I heard Papa's voice. "It's okay, Charity, we're here. You can't talk—there's a tube down your throat. They've put ointment in your eyes. That's why you can't see very well.

"You were burned very badly, and you're in the hospital in Baton Rouge. We have so many questions, but we know you can't talk.

"Roseanna is here at the hospital as well. She was burned too. She's hurting a lot, but she's okay. She explained that you went to Rouses to get cash at the ATM, then you were driving down Martin Luther King Blvd and lost control of the car. Did you blow a tire?"

He tried to make his questions require "yes" or "no" answers so I could nod or shake my head. But some answers weren't always easy. The truth was I couldn't tell him that I didn't know why the car jerked to the left—maybe I hit standing water, perhaps I did blow a tire.

I wanted to see Roseanna. I needed to hear her voice. Was she really ok?

As if telepathically communicating our mutual need to see each other, she came and stood in the doorway. "Hi Charity, I'm here. They won't let me come in. They're afraid we'll infect each other. I love you."

The days after the accident blurred together.

I remember my best friend visiting me, crying the whole time. Afterward, my mom gently explained why my friend was so upset. "Charity, you don't look like yourself." That was true. I was unrecognizable; my body was swollen, my head the size of a basketball.

My boyfriend, Don, had come to visit. He tried to be positive and hopeful. Roseanna told me she remembers her band instructor visiting. Whenever I was awake, my parents told me what was happening.

At one point, Mama told me, "Papa called his parents and asked them to come help with Christy and Clay. They are on their way. I didn't think we needed your Granny and Grandpa (her parents) to come, but when we called them, Granny was very upset. She's catching the next flight out here.

"My dad is going to drive here after he finds someone to take care of the dogs.

"Miss Connie, from church, has called several times. She has you on the prayer chain. There are so many people praying for you and Roseanna. They're also taking food to the house. Papa had to go back home to be with Christy and Clay, but he'll be back tomorrow."

That weekend passed in a haze.

One day early the next week, I woke up, and both my parents were there. Papa explained matter of factly, "Charity, we have some news. Your Grandpa Martin has a cousin who's a Shriner—they're the people who wear funny hats in parades.

The Shriners have a top-rated children's hospital that specializes in burn injuries. Grandpa's cousin called the Shriners Hospital for Children in Galveston, and they happen to have two beds available. They have invited you and Roseanna to take these beds.

"As you are seventeen years old, we feel you should have a say in your medical care. If you choose to accept the Shriners' invitation, they will take care of you and Roseanna free of charge. They can come as early as tomorrow. A team will transport you and Roseanna in a special jet outfitted to take care of you while you travel. Mama would fly with you and stay at the hospital while I take care of things at home and continue working. I'll come to visit you on the weekends when I can. Do you think it's a good idea for you and Roseanna to go to the Shriners Hospital?"

I nodded. I didn't know the difference between that hospital and this one, but I did know that free medical care would help my parents, especially with the two of us in the hospital.

A FEW FACTS ABOUT BURNS

- Your skin is the largest organ of your body. It is the first line of defense against injury, bacteria, germs, and infection; it insulates your body and regulates your temperature.

- There are three layers of skin before the dermis layer—which is the layer that attaches your skin to your muscle.

- The first two layers of skin reproduce themselves every seven days or so.

- The third layer contains your pores and hair follicles.
  - It does not reproduce itself.

- When a person endures a third-degree burn, they no longer have sweat glands or the ability to grow hair.

- Doctors must replace the damaged or missing skin with what is called *donor* skin.

  - The donor cannot be another person.

  - A donor site is an unburned area of the patient's body. Skin is taken from that area to graft onto the area that needs it.

  - In some cases, doctors use pigskin or cadaver skin to cover the affected area. This serves as temporary skin until replacement skin has grown in a skin bank or skin from a donor site is available.

After a donor site has healed, skin can be retaken from that site to cover the injured area.

LOOKING BACK

It feels like this all happened a lifetime ago, or as if it's someone else's story—probably because I am a different person from who I was then. Most years, as the anniversary rolls around, I remember the day, the event, the moment my life spun in a whole new direction. And I'm okay. It feels like just another date on the calendar now, a day I need to work or remember to go to the grocery store. I make a mental note of the day, think of how far I've come, and move on.

Maybe because of losses our family has endured more recently, but lately, I remember more. These days, I look at the whole experience differently. I recognize a single day on the calendar can't mark all that happened the night of the accident.

> IT FEELS LIKE THIS ALL HAPPENED A LIFETIME AGO, OR AS IF IT'S SOMEONE ELSE'S STORY

The results of a split-second decision impacted innumerable people for an immeasurable amount of time.

I remind myself this isn't only my story, but it's theirs, too—my sisters', my parents', my grandparents', my brother's, and my friends'. They were the ones watching, waiting, helping, hoping, and praying. None of them knew if I would live to see the end of that day, much less my graduation. Some had an idea of a future struggle I wasn't even aware of yet. They could see that if I did survive, my life was going to be extraordinarily challenging. My family and friends experienced the horrors resulting from our accident each time they saw me suffering or heard me cry. Under the fog of medication and pain, I was barely aware of what was going on around me.

And, of course, my loved ones felt the stark reality of the potential loss they might have to face. I didn't know my life was hanging in the balance—and if I had any inkling, I didn't contemplate that it was, partially, up to me whether I lived or died. All I knew was I was alive, so my job was to get better.

I have mixed feelings about the incident and my life afterward. Part of me looks back over the past two decades and feels sorrow for what that seventeen-year-old—that other me—survived. I have endured years of pain and loss on many levels—fighting, striving, enduring, waiting, and persevering. There have been times when I felt hopeless, alone, forgotten, fearful, and tormented. It hasn't been easy, and I ache for that girl.

The other side of me looks back and sees victories, triumphs, love, miracles, opportunities, wisdom, compassion, grace, favor, strength, courage, and new life that has emerged from the tragedy. I feel full and want to burst with thankfulness for the goodness of my life.

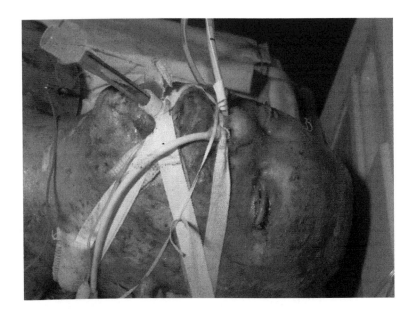

I laid in the hospital bed for more than two months, barely able to move, bandaged from head to foot, fighting through the pain that consumed every movement. I had no clue about the particular challenges my future would hold. I knew my burns were severe. I couldn't perceive how permanent and life-altering the damage was. Logically, I knew it would take a lot of work and time to recover my strength and independence. For goodness' sake, I couldn't even feed myself. But at the time, I focused on getting better, not on what my life—or body—would look like later.

The doctors told me frankly that my skin would never look as it did before, there would be years of surgeries, and my fingers would need to be amputated.

Everyone who entered the room loved me, regardless of how I looked. The hospital staff knew how to see a person for who they were, not how they looked. So, in my mind, the way I saw myself in my mind was exactly as I had last seen myself in the mirror when I checked my makeup and hair before getting into the car. That was the only way I knew myself; it was the "normal" my mind registered. I imagined being burned meant having black soot on me. I knew life had changed, but I couldn't understand how those changes would affect me.

The time in the hospital was rough. It was eye-opening. I had never even visited a hospital before, and now I was among the sickest patients there. A constant string of doctors, nurses, and strangers, entered my room, looked at my body, and commented on my injuries. There was no way I could hide from their inspection. I went from being a girl who preferred to go unnoticed, someone who didn't want to stand out and lived her life to avoid embarrassment at all costs, to someone in the spotlight, naked, vulnerable, and needy. There was absolutely nothing I could do to cover up. I couldn't run away from it, and I couldn't dress myself up to look better. I was raw. I had no secrets; every bodily function was everybody's business. The accident had flipped my life upside down.

I don't know how my family did it. They worked as a unified team. My grandparents immediately came from Arizona to Louisiana when they heard about the accident. They took their posts. Both grandmothers and Grandpa Freeland were at home to care for Clay and Christina. They made it possible for my mama to be in Galveston with Roseanna and me at the hospital. Pregnant with our baby sister, Mom went back and forth between Roseanna's and my rooms. Her father became her constant companion and bodyguard. When Mom was with me, he would sit with Zanna and vice versa.

Papa had to continue to work and be home for Christy and Clay, but he drove six hours to be with me as often as possible. Additionally, everybody took turns coming to visit and shouldered the effort of learning the wound care necessary to help Zanna and me continue to heal once we went home.

We each learned that as a family, we were capable of doing much more than any one of us could alone. We also came to a deeper level of understanding of what is essential in life. All of us have opinions, and we may strongly disagree about details.

At times, we may even be concerned about letting one another down. But we knew that those opinions and fears mattered little compared to the value we placed on each other and life.

At the age of seventeen, I was sure my parents didn't understand me. I knew there were things about which we would never agree. There were situations I had gotten myself into that had the potential for life-changing consequences. When I thought about how my family might respond to those possible scenarios, I was sure they would have been furious and disappointed. I feared that, if they ever found out, they would have left me alone to handle things too big for me, disconnected from their lives. In that frame of mind, I began to truly understand why some teenagers make extreme and devastating choices, whether it be running away, taking drugs, or even committing suicide.

After the accident, I saw how my family handled the tragedy—how they each stepped in and did whatever was necessary for everyone's health and well-being.

I could see more clearly, and I slowly came to understand that no problem could ever be worth losing a life over.

Parents would rather have their child alive, even if there are significant challenges to face and work through, as in times of anger, hurt, confusion, and disappointment, than to have a gravesite to visit.

In the span of a lifetime, most problems are temporary. Some may alter our course, but we get to choose whether they will extinguish our future potential and purpose.

2

CHOICES

My dad is an airplane mechanic and inspector; he went wherever there was work. As a result, we moved around a lot growing up. In our early years, moving didn't bother me. We were all in it together, and we didn't know a different life. Our moves took us to Arizona, Maryland, Venezuela, Texas, Louisiana, and, eventually, Colorado. As we reached middle school and high school, the moves became more challenging as we left behind friends, sports teams, activities, churches, and our communities. We had to start over with the awkward feeling of not knowing where anything was and not having any friends. Rebuilding our lives so often resulted in no one knowing who we were. It seemed we just had time to get established, and then we had to start all over somewhere else.

Our grandparents visited us every summer. They took us camping and swimming, taught us card games and crafts, and shared many life lessons with us. My dad's parents moved quite a bit when he was growing up, so they understood how moving could be complicated.

I recall sharing with my grandparents the woes of moving—again. "I just got on the dance team at the high school. I like going to football games and dancing during half-time; there will be competitions in the spring. I feel like I am a part of something. I don't want to move in the middle of the school year. How am I going to be able to get on the dance team at my new school and cheer for another football team? That feels disloyal. Why can't my parents just let me stay here until the end of my sophomore year? I'm sure some friends will let me stay with them."

Grandpa heard me out and then offered this advice, "When you move, you need to tell yourself that the new town you're going to is the best place. If you always look at the last home as the best, you'll never see the good things waiting for you. There are always good things to look forward to. It's all about how you look at it. You get to choose your attitude toward life."

* * *

During my recovery in the hospital, I was so sick and felt incapable of anything. Repetition filled my days—baths, debridement (wound treatment), dressing changes, and therapy—day after endless day. People rotated through my room at all hours, making sure I had the meds I needed, helping me with every single movement.

One thing I *could* do was make some choices for myself:

- What meal I wanted to eat.

- Whether I wanted the nurse to grind up my meds or I wanted to attempt to swallow those huge pills whole.

- Whether I wanted white milk or chocolate milk.

- How I treated others.

- What kind of attitude I would have.

- To be angry, bitter, resentful, and selfish, or kind, caring, and compassionate.

- To consider my life over or doomed to failure.

- To only see my problems.

- To see others and what they were going through to care for me.

- Whether to complain, whine, and groan my way through every task.

- To push through and do what my doctors and therapists told me to do.

- To make this whole thing easier or more difficult for those around me.

- To be angry at God for allowing such a terrible thing to happen to us.

- To see the miracles
  - in the way God saved me from the car;
  - that the sky cleared just long enough to take us by helicopter to the burn hospital;

- in how I survived the first night and the first few weeks;

- that we had the best doctors, nurses, and treatment facilities—for free;

- and that Roseanna and I had the gift of a family and friends who loved us, prayed for us, and took care of every single thing we needed.

- To see God as distant, uncaring, or even non-existent, or to see God as the One who rescued us—Our Savior—and trust He must have done so for some unknown purpose.

Even amid my treatments, surgeries, and recovery, I could make decisions about the person I wanted to become due to this life-changing trauma.

The doctors explained how difficult the years ahead would be. Countless surgeries were to come, procedures that could never fully restore what I had lost. Impairments would need to be accommodated. There was unknown emotional and psychological damage, a natural result of trauma, along with the social and developmental disruptions that come with burn injuries and disfigurement.

Realizing that I didn't want to be the physical and emotional mess the doctors predicted, I decided to prove I was different. I could still have a full, healthy, active life doing all the things a typical young adult would do.

It was going to be a lot of hard work, and I knew I needed help. This challenge was far too big for me. I needed God on my side—so I chose to see Him as my Savior, my Healer, and my closest Friend. I could not afford to make Him my enemy. Without His help, I had no hope for anything good to come out of this new reality I faced.

"What, then, shall we say in response to these things? If God is for us, who can be against us? He who did not spare his own Son, but gave him up for us all—how will he not also, along with him, graciously give us all things? Who will bring any charge against those whom God has chosen?" (Romans 8:31-33 NIV)

* * *

When I climbed into the car that rainy night in January, I was young, beautiful, full of life, full of dreams, confident with my hands and their agility. I was even getting along with my family. I knew I was doing my best in every area of my life; I was content, and I was happy.

Someone else rolled out of the car that night.

I didn't have any idea how bad I looked. I imagined that my burned skin looked something like being covered in charcoal or perhaps blisters. The black would wash off, the blisters would heal, and eventually, I would move on with life. It didn't occur to me that I could lose my face, fingers, ability to function, plans, and dreams for the future. I had no inkling that I was unrecognizable, and it would make others sick to see me. That night I went from Beauty to Beast.

The girl who climbed into the car was gone. There was someone else in her place. I lost a measure of my youth that night, and with it, the ability to be carefree and silly; life wasn't funny now. It was serious. The fragility of life impressed upon me. Petty things no longer mattered.

There have been days I've grieved over the loss of that girl. I look at my childhood pictures and see that girl didn't get to finish growing up. They stop with the senior photos taken two months before the accident.

What would she look like now?

That girl had looked like her grandmother. She had her great-grandfather's hands and her Papa's eyes. But those resemblances were gone now. There was somebody else in her place, answering to her name—like "Invasion of the Body Snatchers" except in reverse. I was now in someone else's body.

As the months and years passed, there were many times I wanted to wake from this living nightmare. The brutal dream that left me entirely dependent upon others caused me excruciating pain every day, required I relearn the most basic of functions, and sent me to surgery after surgery—none of them recovering who I once was. In this state, I had to find a way to love this person I had become and believe others could love her too.

How I longed to wake up wiser and stronger from my life-like dream to continue with my plans. But this wasn't a dream; it was my reality. And my life, interrupted and scarred in so many ways, was what I had left. God had chosen to let me live. My choice, therefore, was to press through my loss and do the best I could with what I had. And that was something I'd always done.

Growing up, we didn't have money for extreme home makeovers. We moved from one rental home to another. We didn't have the option to paint the walls or change the flooring and fixtures. We couldn't buy new decorative items every three years when the trends changed. I enjoyed going through my mama's linens and knick-knacks to find new ways to display them. I would rearrange the rooms and reorganize the closets for fun. I found satisfaction in the challenge of making the most of what we had.

Now my challenge wasn't what I would do with my bedroom, but what I could do with my life.

I remember when my parents told me the doctors had to amputate the fingers on my right hand. These fingers were a part of me that loved to draw and create things. They were fingers that could untie any knot and extend to meeting a new person. They were perfect fingers.

My response? "Well, I'll have to learn to write with my left hand."

I can't say that I wasn't upset at losing them. After the surgery, I laid in my bed for two days, thinking my fingers were still attached. I could feel them there. Maybe the miracle we were praying for happened!

When I finally got the nerve to ask about my hand, however, my parents confirmed that the surgeon had taken my fingers away.

The physical pain of losing my fingers kept me awake at night. No medication could relieve it. It was a different kind of pain than the burns, nerves, bone, and tissue left raw and exposed. Sometimes, I can still remember the agony today. Once in a while, when I'm overtired or emotional, and my little hand slips off of a drawer or door handle, it hurts. You might find me jumping up and down, hurt and frustrated that I have to deal with that loss and pain again, which is now nothing compared to what it was then.

LIFE AND DEATH

"Now what I am commanding you today is not too difficult for you or beyond your reach. No, the word is very near you; it is in your mouth and in your heart so you may obey it. This day I call the heavens and the earth as witnesses against you that I have set before you life and death, blessings and curses.

Now choose life, so that you and your children may live and that you may love the LORD your God, listen to his voice, and hold fast to him. For the LORD is your life..." (Deuteronomy 30:11, 14, 19-20 NIV)

An angel led the way. It didn't wear the traditional white robe or have wings protruding from its back. I can't say whether it was female or male, but I knew it was an angel, a servant sent to take me to Jesus. We wound our way through a maze-like course, then approached a gallery. It was full of abstract paintings (my favorite). Some looked vaguely familiar. "These are amazing!" I exclaimed. I thought, *I wonder if I can copy these? That would probably be illegal—plagiarism.* We didn't linger long.

The angel took me into a room, but it wasn't enclosed. White columns protruded from the four corners of the floor, but there was no ceiling. Vines wound their way up Romanesque columns. The room wasn't attached to a building. It seemed to hover in the clouds, infiltrated by light.

In the middle of the room, I saw a white coffin. I somehow understood this coffin was for me—but white? I wasn't pure. I hadn't kept my life clean and innocent as a child. I stood next to it with Jesus by my side. He seemed familiar, like a close friend, and I felt peaceful standing next to Him. I absorbed the beauty, light, and mystery of the place. "It's so beautiful here; I want to stay forever! But, if You want me to, I'll go back."

* * *

I woke up in recovery after yet another surgery. The doctors had terminated the procedure when my blood pressure dropped *deathly* low. Having returned from my heavenly detour, I felt compelled to pray for my family. In my heart, I prayed for their pain, heartache, and weariness. I prayed for those that did not have a relationship with God. There was no denying the reality of Jesus; I had just seen Him! Even after the nurse rolled me into my room, where Christy waited for me, I could still feel angelic beings surrounding me. "Jesus, Jesus, Jesus…"—spoken in worship and awe—were the only words I could form.

One year earlier, I had denied the God I had known since I was a small child. I chose to do my own thing. I wanted to learn my way. I told Him, "You have too many rules. You must not have meant them for me. I'm tired of trying to be perfect all the time; I'm tired of being *naïve*." I behaved foolishly. My rebellion put my life and the lives of others at risk.

The guilt I felt weighed heavily on my teenage heart, and I was constantly afraid someone would catch me doing things I knew I shouldn't. I'm sure the shame was evident on my face when a family friend who had come to visit us from Texas said to me, "Charity, I know what you are doing. God told me. You'd better get it straight with Him. He is not happy."

A few weeks after that warning, I had a nightmare of plummeting within a bottomless hole. I knew where I was going. Fear overwhelmed me. When I woke up, I was relieved to discover it had been a dream—and another warning.

Shortly after that revelation, my friend Jenny came to me and declared, "Charity, you *have* to come to church with me tonight!" She had just been saved. The church was showing the production, "Heaven's Gates or Hell's Flames"—a drama that portrayed eternity both in heaven and in hell. It addressed common beliefs about death and sin and ended with the question, "If you die tomorrow, where will you go?" After watching it, I knew the only way I would feel peace again was to recommit my life to God. I asked for His forgiveness. I pledged my life to Him. I spent the next few months trying to untangle the messes I had made in my rebellion.

I laid in my hospital bed, reminiscing of my trip to heaven. I had never dreamed before in any of my other surgeries. Anesthesia knocks me out; I wake up after hours-long surgery in what feels like moments. I reckon I must have died. I thought about the gallery I had seen in my dream. *No wonder it's taking so long for Jesus to come back.* I thought. *He's making heaven for each one of us.* Reliving the joy and the peace made me feel at home—there, I was beautiful again. There, I could walk or fly without pain. But God decided for me to return here. And I let Him make the choice.

"*...I have set before you life and death...Now choose life...*"(Deuteronomy 30:19 NIV)

I didn't know the impact that choice would make. How could I? I was only seventeen, and while I grew up with biblical teachings, there was no way I could have been trained on how to respond if you die and are given a choice to live on Earth or stay in heaven.

When I said to Jesus, "*...not my will, but Yours be done...*" *(Luke 22:42 NIV),* it was as if He poured the gift of grace on me.

Grace doesn't make everything easy. The gift simply and inexplicably makes the impossible possible. The peace I received that day stayed with me, giving me the inner strength to endure another dressing change, the resolve to push through another therapy session, and the tenacity to try again, in a new way, when the old way was no longer an option.

> GRACE DOESN'T MAKE EVERYTHING EASY. THE GIFT SIMPLY AND INEXPLICABLY MAKES THE IMPOSSIBLE POSSIBLE.

Grace gave me the strength to decide what to believe and how I would respond to life:

- God is good, no matter how my life and future look.

- I would ride in cars (and wear my seatbelt), and I would drive again.

- Fire would not scare me.

- People talking about fire, accidents, or burns would not trigger me, and others would not walk on eggshells around me.

- I would not be bitter or angry.

These decisions were the beginning of choosing life. In the years that followed, grace gave me the nuggets of revelation and truth I would need for each step of the journey:

- Grace gave me compassion for others—wisdom and insight into their pain.

- Grace gave words of encouragement.

- Grace had repeatedly given me the strength to stick with my choices, even on the hardest of days, when I wanted to give up.

Because of grace, I choose life. And life has endless possibilities.

* * *

When I'm in my deepest pain, doubt comes flooding in about God and His love and care for me. When I am hurting the most, it is hard to grab hold of a God who is so big that I can't always see Him and who is so close that I can't always feel Him.

When I find myself asking, "Why did this happen to me?" I choose to answer the question with the answer. So God can be glorified in my life. Subsequently, He can heal me at deeper levels, teach me incredible things, and reveal Himself in miraculous ways in my life.

When I live with a continual awareness of many others enduring trauma, accidents, abuse, pain, loss, and injustice, I understand these are tragedies and horrors nobody "deserves." Problems seem to happen whether we are "good" or "bad," whatever our station in life, regardless of our beliefs. Why would I imagine awful things could happen to others but not to me?

In some cases, it may seem God was absent in a tragedy. I choose to see Him as being present in the healing—recognizing that without Him, there is no true healing.

I recognize that regardless of the present circumstances, tremendous losses, and the messiest seasons, God is good even if things don't turn out the way I wanted.

Then I choose life.

If I answer the "why" question saying that

- God is unfair or unjust.

- He is punishing me.

- He wasn't there.

Then, I am choosing a type of death. I blame Him for my misfortunes as though I deserve more than what He has already given me—life. I believe lies about His character and His plans for me.

> *"For I know the plans I have for you, declares the* LORD, *plans to prosper you and not to harm you, plans to give you hope and a future." (Jeremiah 29:11 NIV)*

When I blame him, I am questioning His motivation as anything other than love for me. All of these lines of reasoning put me at odds with God. They cause me to distance my heart, mind, and emotions from the One who can heal, comfort, and give me peace.

Sometimes, it feels easier to choose death. In death, there can be an immediate end to the present pain. Ending one's own life is much broader than physical death or suicide.

CHOOSING DEATH

When I give up,
When I make declarations stating
    I will never;
    I will not;
    you can't make me,
When I let
    fear dictate my future,
    and negative words shape my destiny.
I am placing bars around my cell;
    calling it "safe,"
    where no more pain or trauma can touch me,
I am
    controlling my future;
    limiting my options;
    filtering out the possible paths;
    and making my life map small.
I am
    requiring everyone who cares about me to bow
    to my pain,
    trapping them in my circumstances.
Choosing death
    denies creativity;
    leaves no room for faith;
    snuffs out hope;
    pushes away grace;
    leaves me all alone;
    fuels my fears;
    and confines me to my worst pain.

* * *

As I lay in my hospital room, my mom often prayed, sang, read, and spoke Scripture. One quote she said over and over was,

"I would have lost heart unless I had believed That I would see the goodness of the LORD In the land of the living." (Psalm 27:13 NKJV)

Choosing life was easier than I thought. Yes, it's filled with unknowns, trials, and pain. It also has surprises, celebrations, joy, and love. Sometimes choosing life is about the simple things:

- listening to someone else's bad day instead of spouting off on my own.

- talking to a child and imagining life through their eyes.

- speaking positive, hopeful words.

- getting up and doing the hard things.

- saying "yes" to opportunities—especially the ones that challenge me.

- making sure those closest to me know they are loved.

- being thankful.

- dreaming.

I often imagine God in heaven, His angels all around, looking at us and cheering us on to "Choose life! Choose life! Choose life!"

THE POWER OF WORDS

It was our first Christmas after the accident. Daniel and Judy were family friends who had come to visit us from Texas. They were like an uncle and aunt to me. Whenever they were around, we all joked and laughed a lot. One day, we were hanging out on the porch and everyone started sharing memories and funny stories of the past. Daniel told a story about me when I was twelve years old. Our family had gone over to their house for a Saturday barbeque. Their home sat at the top of a grassy hill. I had saved all my babysitting money to buy a pair of white overall shorts, and I wore them proudly that day. All of us kids were running and playing outside, until I tripped and went sliding down the hill, scuffing my knee. I got up and went into the house, tears streaming down my face. After the adults checked me over and determined the damage to my knee didn't merit the tears, someone asked why I was crying. "Because my overalls are grass-stained! They're ruined!"

The household erupted in laughter at the memory, but I wasn't laughing. To everyone else, those overalls were merely a piece of clothing and my response seemed overly-dramatic. Even years later, I remembered how I had worked and saved to buy them. I had seen them as my ticket to fitting in at school. When everyone laughed at Daniel's retelling of the story, their joy seemed at the cost of my misfortune, and it stung. I attempted to redirect the focus of the conversation. "What happened to you, Daniel? It seems that you have more hair on your face these days than on the top of your head!" I quipped.

Suddenly, the laughter died down, and the conversation shifted awkwardly to another topic.

Later in the day, Daniel gently pulled me aside and said, "Charity, you may think you're just a kid, and that what you say doesn't matter. You may even think there's no way your words could hurt someone like me. But you need to know—your words hurt."

This time, my rebuttal to his story stung him. I had wrapped my "perceived truth" in a joke and thought I was simply giving back what had been dished out. But that wasn't the case. Daniel's story about me was about my dramatic response to a ruined piece of clothing. In return, I pointed out something that Daniel saw as a personal flaw, something over which he had no control. My joke intentionally touched on his insecurity, and everyone knew it.

"I'm sorry; I thought we all were joking around," I said.

"We were, but you crossed the line, and you need to know even at your young age, your words have power."

* * *

When thinking about life choices, I can't help but consider the effects of my words.

As we were growing up, we had two ideologies regarding words, especially those Mama allowed us to speak. Our mama valued words. She loved to read and write and devoted her time to studying Scripture. She encouraged anyone who wandered onto her path. She was full of joy, faith, and love. She carefully chose her children's names, intentionally relating their meanings and messages. Her words influenced some type of destiny over other peoples' lives, and she lived acutely aware of the power that words hold.

> *"The tongue has the power of life and death, and those who love it will eat its fruit." (Proverbs 18:21 NIV)*

> *"With the tongue we praise our Lord and Father, and with it we curse human beings, who have been made in God's likeness. Out of the same mouth come praise and cursing." (James 3:9-10 NIV)*

Our dad was brilliant and a smart aleck. He played with words and their meanings. He loved to have the last word and always enjoyed harassing people, including banter and joking around. He thrived on the game of wits involved. He could also be less filtered in his conversations.

While our mama loved to laugh and play, she didn't like joking, as it could lead to saying mean things to other people in the name of "play." As I stated before, she was cautious about what she spoke and recognized that words had the power to build people up or tear them down.

On the one hand, Papa encouraged us to have witty, smart come-backs. If they stung the other person a bit—no big deal—that was part of the game. On the other hand, Mama didn't allow us to call each other names or declare others—their choices (or their food creations) to be dumb, stupid, disgusting, or gross. When we attempted to speak to our parents with disrespect or an elevated tone, they swiftly corrected us.

For a long time, I didn't understand why we couldn't talk how I heard my peers talking; I didn't understand why my mom would get so upset when we were joking. Now I realize our version of joking was harsh, using truth wrapped in a sarcastic tone to get away with saying what we wouldn't otherwise be allowed.

Why couldn't we make digs at our siblings' weaknesses? It felt good to fight sometimes and better to win. I didn't understand the power within the words. I never realized I could hurt other people, even adults, with my jokes.

* * *

With His words, God spoke creation into existence. His words are living and active; they guide us in truth and love, and they build us up and declare our future. His words heal, set people free, transform minds, and change hearts. They are the vehicle through which His love travels.

Just as words built the foundations of the universe, words have the power to destroy. Jesus cursed a fig tree, and it died. He talked to demons, and they scattered. He spoke to disease, and it disappeared. When God made me in His image, He gave me the same power to build up or tear down with my words—just as I could choose life or death.

I can choose to speak my words in faith or fear.

- Will they be full of potential or with limitations?
- Will I fight for freedom, healing, and truth, or my comfort and selfish desires?
- Will I speak the truth in love?
- Will I fuel fear?
- Will I protect myself by tearing others down?
- Will I build others up, helping them to see their worth?
- Will I point them to Jesus?

It's always unbelievable to me—the power God has entrusted to us. He encourages us, "Choose Life!"

"Don't use foul or abusive language. Let everything you say be good and helpful, so that your words will be an encouragement to those who hear them." (Ephesians 4:29 NLT)

I understand now why my mama cringed when she heard us saying ugly things to each other. Her heart hurt when the children she loved were abusing each other. She understood our words were shaping each other's outlooks on life.

Words are the way we communicate with God in prayer. I think of the power of Mama's supplications as she sat by our bedsides in the hospital and the hope she held close to her heart regardless of the negative words of doctors, friends, and family. I think about what she allowed my ears to hear and how she shielded me. I think about how intricately woven those words were to her—the mustard seed of faith that moves mountains.

Treasures in the Trials

At the Shriners Hospital, they do not let you look at yourself in the mirror until your life is no longer in danger, and they think you can handle it emotionally. I asked to look in the mirror early on, but they didn't let me. They've discovered that many people with facial burns, especially teenagers, will not choose to fight for their survival once they see another face staring back at them from the mirror.

The staff members were careful to keep mirrors out of my room. However, about two weeks before I was to go home when they had me up and practicing how to walk, I wandered into the private bathroom attached to my room. I looked in the mirror and what I saw wasn't the reflection I had grown accustomed to throughout my life. The person looking back at me resembled a little old man, bald and discolored, as if I had been beaten up. The alien image was verging on *ET*. I took in the disturbing, intriguing, visual image—it was unreal. I looked nothing like how I pictured myself.

I'm sure you would expect that I started crying and screaming, horrified by what I saw, but I didn't. The tears came later. And there would be plenty of them as it took years to become accustomed to the fact that the person staring back at me when I looked in the mirror was me. Someday I would need to like who I saw.

At the time, all I knew was what I had seen in movies when people had horrific things happen to them. In a few of these stories, people overcame their disabilities and went on to do incredible things. Most films portrayed those with disabilities as angry, bitter victims who hid themselves away, secretly longing to feel loved, but rejecting people before they could feel rejected. These actors portrayed people who had flashbacks to their accidents. Certain words might tip them off. Anyone allowed to be around them had to walk on eggshells. They were real-life examples of "the Beast."

I knew I didn't want that to be my life. If that's how I was supposed to react, if that's what the world expected of me, then I couldn't do it. For some reason, I was alive, and that meant I had a lot of years still in front of me. I couldn't live all those years as a monster.

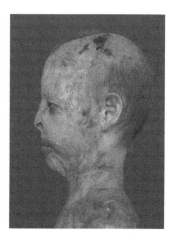

* * *

Surviving, overcoming, and thriving are all choices. Regardless of what life throws at us—the good and the bad—we get to decide what we're going to do with it. Repeatedly, we hear the adage, "When life gives you lemons, make lemonade." But we don't learn how to make a delicious beverage or a beautiful life until we've tasted the sourness and worked hard to sweeten it.

> WE DON'T LEARN HOW TO MAKE A DELICIOUS BEVERAGE OR A BEAUTIFUL LIFE UNTIL WE'VE TASTED THE SOURNESS AND WORKED HARD TO SWEETEN IT.

I believe a large part of thriving has to do with outlook. The doctors informed my family and me that many people who sustain this degree of injury do not survive. They also told us that teenagers, especially girls, often don't make it. They *choose* death. They don't want to face life with scars. The pain is too much, so they don't fight to live.

I never really saw myself as resilient, a fighter, or even particularly willful. I was quiet, shy, and easy-going. I lost most fights with my sisters because I'd give up; I'd get tired of arguing. Hearing the doctors' words, I knew I wouldn't choose the easy way out. I had already seen how untimely death hurt my family.

When I was five years old, we lost a family member—an uncle, my dad's brother, and my grandparents' son. Todd was only seventeen. He tried to solve problems he had gotten himself into on his own. Todd didn't want to disappoint his parents or ruin his future. He didn't get help, and he didn't know what the ramifications of his actions would be. The cost was Todd's life, and it left a huge hole in our family.

While I wasn't going to give up, I can't say I knew how to move forward. I had never imagined myself facing a debilitating injury. Like most people, I hadn't thought through how fragile life was and how quickly any of our lives can change. There wasn't much I could do lying in a bed, entirely dependent, waiting for surgeries to help me heal, working through the pain. As stated earlier, I could choose my attitude, words, and perspective. That's about all I could do.

People often regarded my mama as an idealist. She could find the good in every person she came across. She saw everything around her through the lens of faith and hope. She was joyful and bubbly, and she dreamed big dreams.

On the other hand, our papa bordered on pessimism, though he preferred to call it realism. We nicknamed him "Eeyore." When we phoned him to ask him how he was doing, "Fair to partly cloudy" was his typical response. He called it as he saw it.

As you can imagine, this mixture of parental personalities would produce some unique children. I tend to think of myself as a hopeful realist. I go about life pretty pragmatically, with a lot of faith mixed in. I want to know how to live the Word of God in real-time.

One of the ways I've held onto believing in the impossible and trusting in miracles—while still having to walk through pain—is to look for little treasures. If God is living and active, if He is concerned about every detail of my itty-bitty life, if He is indeed my Rescuer, my Comforter, and my Healer, then I need to see where He is working. Otherwise, the misery, darkness, doubt, and future are way too overwhelming.

* * *

When the Israelites crossed the Jordan into the promised land, they built an altar. They put down "Stones of Remembrance" to recall the miraculous works God had done on their behalf while leading them into freedom. The stones were a marker for generations to follow. No matter what life looks like, God is real, and we are His people.

As my family members shared our information around the accident, trying to piece the whole story together, we discovered treasures like stones of remembrance. We started seeing people positioned in the right places, at the perfect times, to help us along the way. They took us to the places we couldn't get to on our own and helped us when we weren't able to help ourselves. Therefore, we saw them as gifts—divine gifts.

We noted treasured conversations with other parents and nurses about their struggles. Our hospital rooms held hope and peace, whereas most other rooms remained filled with fear and grief. Our recovery steps went a smidge faster than usual. We had a support system many others envied. In the most painful of times, we could honestly say we were blessed.

It would have been easy to count up our losses, tally the distress load, and forecast a doomed future filled with surgeries, scars, and stares. But we found it was unrealistic to paint that picture without adding in the light. Yes, there was profound loss, ample work to do, and plenty to grieve, but there was a plethora to be thankful for too. Those positive things were essential to my progression.

That's what I thrived on for years—the little victories that kept me moving forward. Looking for treasures in the trials became a genuine necessity. It proved to be a strong foundation—one that supports me in not being angry with God when bad things happen. Whether it was having a rough day in therapy or further down the road when our family encountered floods, miscarriages, bypass surgeries, heartbreaks, divorces, cancer diagnoses, and the losses of our closest loved ones, there is always a gem—deposited by God—to be uncovered, if I take the time to look for it.

3

HEALING

The view from my bed was of walls, hallways, elevators, and masked faces. After arriving at Shriners Hospital for Children the first day, attendants parked me in my room and transferred me to my bed. Immediately a nurse came in.

"Hi, Charity; welcome. We're going to take good care of you. Are you doing okay?" she inquired.

I nodded. I was as "okay" as I could be; the attendants had all worked hard to make my journey comfortable; I didn't want to cause further inconvenience. Transfers hurt, but nobody was touching me right now, and the hospital staff here was communicating with me. I didn't remember them doing that in the other hospital.

She must have seen distress register across my face, regardless of my response. "We're getting you some pain medicine right away; we want you to be as comfortable as possible. As soon as we can, we're going to get that tube out of you so you can talk again. You'd like that, wouldn't you?"

I nodded and tried to smile.

"Well, I'm going to go make sure your medicine is ordered." She must have pointed to a button on the bed rail, maybe even a remote on the bedside table, but I really couldn't see anything. My hands were bandaged, hurt so badly I wouldn't have been able to grasp anything offered to me. "Whenever you need anything at all, just call," my nurse said.

Before the accident, I had never been to a hospital before, not even to visit anyone. I had never broken a bone or experienced any health issue beyond having the flu. I didn't know hospital rooms had call buttons. In any case, I could not have pushed them in my condition. In the days and weeks that followed, whenever I needed the nurse, I barked in my scratchy whisper, "Nurse . . . nurse . . . nurse . . . " until someone finally heard me and came to help me.

My parents were both there when the doctor came in and introduced himself and then gave a short explanation, "We are the best burn hospital in the country, aggressive in our treatment. Our goal is to get you home quickly, one day in the hospital for every one degree of burn; for example, Roseanna has burns on 30 percent of her body. She should be here for approximately thirty days. Charity, you have burns on 75 percent of your body. We hope to get you home in less than three months. That sounds like a long time, but most adults who have had a burn your size stay in regular burn hospitals for six to eight months."

My injuries started at the top of my head and went to my knees. My feet were the only things that didn't hurt. The doctors were uncertain about my vision. My eyes had some damage, so they kept heavy ointment in them all the time. I couldn't see much. I wasn't able to do anything or go anywhere. The accident had reduced me to complete dependence on others at the age of seventeen years old.

Roseanna's burns were on her back and down her arms. Many of her burns were second-degree, meaning her nerve endings were still intact. She was alert and mobile, despite being in incredible pain—a fact she let everyone know. Zanna is a textbook redhead, a spitfire. While I hated that I hurt her, I was glad to have her close by. When we were admitted, they placed her in the room right next to mine. I didn't like going to new places alone; I was used to always having my sisters around.

One day, my nurse came in. "Charity," she said, "I'm going to explain *debridement* to you. For your wounds to heal, we need to do more than just bathing to keep them clean. Debridement is a time-consuming, detailed procedure where we have to scrub, tweeze, and snip to remove the dead tissue. We know this procedure hurts badly, and we'll try to keep you as comfortable as possible, but if we leave the dead skin there, it can breed infection. If infection sets in, it can quickly go deep into the bone and lead to amputation or death. Infection is our biggest concern."

Each day started with soaking off the bandages that covered our burns. Then the nurse wheeled our beds into the tub room for daily debridement. The nurse was right; it was an excruciating process. My nurse would try to time my pain medication to line up with my tub time, but the medicine didn't stop it from hurting.

As I laid in the tub, I heard the cries and screams of other children going through the same process. I tried the best I could not to cry out. I hated to cry, but I couldn't help it. "Owie, owie, owie, owie, owie…" I would cry out; it was my hint to the nurse that they should stop. But they didn't stop. The debridement sessions seemed unending.

The nurses would do their best to comfort me as they cleaned away the dead skin.

"I know, Charity, I'm sorry. I have to."

"It will be over soon."

"Hang on, Charity."

As time went on and my vision cleared, I noticed tears in my nurse's eyes as she worked. I realized that none of them wanted to hurt me; they were helping me. I thought of the other kids who were too young to understand the burn nurses' and therapists' care and determination. They probably saw their caregivers as the ones causing their pain instead of their injuries.

In the evenings, the bandages they applied after the debridement were soaked off and changed again. The staff taught my parents and grandparents how to wrap us up in ace bandages and recruited them to help with our dressing changes.

I was the most acute patient on the floor, meaning my burns were most extensive. I was very sick and required a lot of work. At least two nurses were in my room at any given time; doctors and residents would make their rounds bringing in eight to ten people. Therapists, psychologists, volunteers, cleaners, visitors, including clowns and the Easter Bunny (it was a children's hospital) circulated throughout the day.

Mama stayed with us day and night. She read to me, prayed with and for me, and kept me company. She also communicated my needs to the staff. Most importantly, Mama constantly spoke hope and life to me—and to anyone with whom she came into contact. The nurses loved her.

Papa came out on weekends. My grandparents visited too. They took turns keeping Roseanna and me entertained—when we were awake and not undergoing some type of treatment. Other visitors came on weekends. Papa would have them come into my room without me noticing. They were to adjust to how I looked, then leave the room and cry, pass out, vomit, whatever. Once their emotions were under control, they would come back in, and he would announce their presence.

* * *

Emotional healing is similar to the debridement process that took place for my physical injury. It hurts to heal. On my journey, there are times when I felt God was going into the most sensitive parts of my heart with His tweezers and plucking the lack of forgiveness, my hatred, anger, fear, lies, and other offense at the source. He knows these unhealthy things must be pulled out or snipped off before they cause infection and affect my whole life.

> *"See to it that no one falls short of the grace of God and that no bitter root grows up to cause trouble and defile many."* *(Hebrews 12:15 NIV)*

It's sobering to realize I can fall short of God's grace. For me, this happens when I get too focused on myself:

- my pain,

- my circumstances;

- when I see lack instead of blessings.

I miss God's grace when I only focus on my present circumstances, forgetting the bigger picture. At those times, I fail to look for the positive things God is doing, how He is caring for my needs—especially when His provision looks nothing like what I asked for or wanted. I begin to doubt, stop believing, and allow a bitter root to sprout up. The crazy thing about bitter roots, they don't just hurt me; they sour those around me.

Decisions in my life do not only affect me— aside from what kind of toothpaste I use. My choices affect those who

> I MISS GOD'S GRACE WHEN I ONLY FOCUS ON MY PRESENT CIRCUMSTANCES, FORGETTING THE BIGGER PICTURE.

love me. For example, when I leave things unresolved or choose to coddle my pain, self-hatred, and lack of forgiveness, that bitter root gets fed. When I justify it and give it space to grow, that sprout will defile many. It can injure those closest to me.

To truly heal, I have to choose to allow God to stifle that bitter root—to go in, touch the broken places, take away the stuff that leads to death and destruction, and pour His balm on the wounded area. In His kindness, He knows that sometimes I have to endure pain to build the capacity to heal. *"Do I have the courage? Do I trust Him?"*

"Come, let us return to the LORD. He has torn us to pieces; now he will heal us. He has injured us; now he will bandage our wounds. In just a short time he will restore us, so that we may live in his presence." (Hosea 6:1-2)

I AM NOT ALONE

After being in the hospital for two and a half months, I was finally released. I walked in the front door of our house after a long ride and exclaimed, "Hi family, I'm home!"

There were so many emotions. My family was excited to have me home; I was ecstatic to be there. We had been preparing for this for weeks now. This was the goal, and we had achieved it.

Clay came running up to me, hugging my knees. He was careful not to touch my bandages. I had missed him so much! It must have been confusing for him when we were suddenly gone.

Roseanna had returned home six weeks earlier. The grandmothers had been doing her wound care and dressing changes; they all had stories to tell. Christina had to grow up fast; the whole family had depended on her to help with Clay and the household chores while keeping up with school. All that on top of adjusting to her sisters and mother being gone for months.

The question running through all of our minds at some level, "We can get back to normal now, can't we?"

AFTER THE ACCIDENT

- I had six surgeries during my initial two and a half months in the hospital. Those were necessary to restore skin over my whole body.

- I was too sick to get up or walk on my own. Every movement hurt. I had therapy every day to stretch my new skin and the forming scars to eventually regain full range of motion.

- Scars want to grow straight, not with the curves of your body.

- Scar tissue does not stretch or bounce back into place like normal skin. Notice how the skin on your elbow expands when you bend it and smooths out when you straighten your arm. When you have scar tissue on your elbow, you have to stretch the skin slowly and repeatedly to allow the elbow to bend. When you straighten a scarred elbow, the stretched skin sags, remaining loose and floppy.

- I had to wear hand splints between therapy sessions continuously, so I wouldn't lose the motion I had gained.

- I wore a collar to form the scars to my neck's shape, so they wouldn't grow straight down from my chin to my chest.

- Another torturous device I required was a mouth spreader to push out the corners of my mouth, so scars didn't grow straight down from cheek to chin, leaving me unable to open my mouth for food or speech.

- A silicone mask was necessary for twenty to twenty-two hours a day for a year. The mask put pressure on my facial scars to soften and flatten them.

- Finally, I sported a Jobst Suit for more than a year. This is a custom garment made from a flat-knit fabric—like very thick stockings. It's crafted to fit snugly from head to toe to keep pressure on all the scars, thereby decreasing the chance of keloid (heavy, thick) scars developing while softening and protecting new fragile skin.

- After being in the hospital for six to eight weeks, my doctors finally allowed me to get out of bed and practice walking, a simple feat that I had to relearn.

- When released from the hospital in April of 1994, I remained unable to accomplish basic tasks like standing or sitting down, dressing or feeding myself, and writing. Nurses came every day to help bathe me and change my bandages.

- When I went home, trays were installed at shoulder height on either side of my bed. They were at ninety-degree angles to the bed so I could sleep with each arm resting on a tray. This way, I wouldn't lose the ability to open my arms while sleeping. Essentially, I slept in the shape of a cross or a "T."

- I went to physical and occupational therapy at least three times a week.

- In May, I attended my graduation and was the maid of honor at my best friend's wedding the next day.

- Throughout the summer, I taught myself to write and draw with my left hand.

- I slowly regained my independence over the next year, pushing myself to get back to what I considered normal.

- We regularly went back to Shriners Hospital six hours away for checkups, supplies, fittings, and surgeries.

- My sister Laura was born in September that year. Her presence brought a welcome distraction from the effects of the injuries. She was life and a cause for celebration in the midst of the struggles.

- In January of 1995, a year after my accident, I had my first of at least twenty reconstructive surgeries that would occur during the next seven years. These surgeries helped my right-hand function, added shape and form through implants, used my existing hair to cover the bald areas on my head, and improved my overall function and appearance.

- In July of 1995, our family moved to Colorado.

- At age nineteen, I was ready to be independent and got my first apartment.

* * *

It's interesting; we often think that they are all better when a person leaves the hospital, that life is looking up; there is no more need for worry. But from my perspective, going home was more challenging than being in the hospital.

I felt like home meant life would be normal again, and the nightmare would be over. In reality, the time in the hospital was the restless sleep before the nightmare. It didn't feel normal to be in the hospital. It wasn't familiar; other people were strangers; I didn't spend days and nights the same way. I didn't ever expect "normal" while I was there.

I worked for, dreamt about, and waited to go home. To go back to the world that was familiar to me, the life I knew, the people I felt the safest with, and the plans that I'd left behind. When I walked through the front door, it was all there, the life I was suspended from for two and a half months.

My baby brother was a little bigger and eager to play. My friends were ready to hang out, and school arranged things to receive me. My family prepared for dinners with everyone sitting around the table. My mom thought she'd send me to the store or have me babysit my brother. My sisters were awaiting their big sister to help them through their teenage years. Colleges were waiting to accept my applications, and my job equipped me to continue my position.

There was one difference—me. I came home a very different person than when I had walked out. My life was no longer hanging in the balance, but nothing was right or normal.

The person who had walked out the door the night of the accident was strong and healthy; she was independent and filled with the hopes and dreams within her grasp. She was months away from graduation and looking forward to the life awaiting her.

When I came home from the hospital, reality hit me. Those hopes and dreams would have to wait. The fire had snatched away the body I was used to—the one that had been sheltered, protected, and trained to be a good and productive member of society—and had replaced it with this one.

This body was missing fingers and was weak. It was ugly—covered in boo-boos, shapeless, and bearing no resemblance to the previous version. The person residing in this body couldn't feed herself; she couldn't stand up or sit down independently; she couldn't bathe or dress herself. This body forced me to start all over again. Nothing was normal.

The following year was a blur of therapy sessions and trips to the hospital for check-ups. I had to wear the mask and pressure garments twenty-three hours a day. Splints, wraps, and various other torturous devices, designed to make my scars softer—and defy their innate character and makeup—created a prison where their captive could not move.

Home health nurses became our best friends; personal care assistants helped my family and me with day-to-day living activities. Little goals became the motivation necessary for me to push through the pain, to reclaim what was threatening to be lost forever.

I learned it was okay to take baby steps. I purchased kindergarten-writing tablets, built-up pencils, coloring books, and crayons for training my left hand to do what my right hand could no longer accomplish.

Every day, I expressed frustration over my loss. Over time, it became every other day, then once a week, or once a month. Now, the disappointment or grief of my loss comes sporadically—a couple of times a year.

I learned to celebrate my victories, no matter how small. Things I never thought to notice in the past: the ability to move my built-up spoon to my mouth, to raise my hand above my head, tie my shoes one-handed, carry a glass, or open the door myself.

In the meantime, there were events like my graduation, weddings, fairs, movies, and shopping. All of these were signs of life. Signs that lives were moving forward. As I participated in each event, my emotions were diametrically opposed.

On one side, I had increased respect for my family and friends; I was ecstatic to be stepping back into life and all it entailed. I loved being a part of things. My friends and family continually showed me how grateful they were that I was alive and making new memories with them.

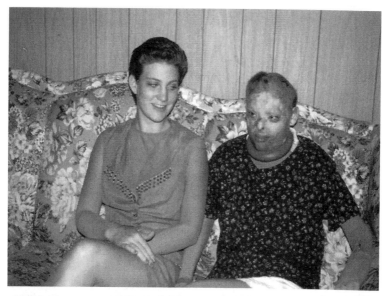

There was also the other side—the incredible grief and sadness. I wasn't at these events in the capacity I should have been. I attended graduation in a mask between my cap and gown, relying on my neighboring classmates to assist me when sitting or standing during the ceremony. I was the maid of honor in my best friend's wedding—an oddity wearing a lacy dress in a beautiful ceremony.

Every "normal" thing I did, especially out in public, carried with it the screaming reminder that no matter how I saw myself, how much I had improved, or how grateful I was, I was not normal. The stares, the comments from onlookers, the questions, the struggle to do the simplest of tasks were a humiliating reminder of my loss. I lost myself.

Bravely, I would muster my strength to step into the spotlight, to perform the most mundane of duties—going to the grocery store—only to return home broken and defeated. I relied on my family and friends to inject the love and encouragement I desperately needed to build up my courage to go out again. They became my source, my lifeline, and my hope that someday it would all be okay.

What I didn't realize was how I was sucking the life out of them. Subtly, the order of our family had shifted. Their days revolved around my mood; their plans ran according to my therapy schedule and doctor's appointments.

All I wanted was to feel like me again. I would search for things to fill the depth of my loss. Each day, I would pick and choose whose company I wanted and who could care for me. Stealthily, selfishness snuck in. I became a jerk, demanding that others do things my way—unaware I was turning into a tyrant. I made my pain theirs and used it to keep my life as comfortable and pain-free as possible. They patiently endured my rants as I consumed everything they had to give, knowing they couldn't give me what I wanted most.

One day, a good family friend showed me how I controlled my family—using my pain and loss to make them conform to my tangled life. When I grasped the notion, I was horrified.

I didn't want to hurt the ones I loved the most. My parents didn't raise me to be the center of the universe. They and my grandparents taught me to be hyper-aware that life wasn't about me and what I wanted; instead, it was about what was best for our family as a whole. Everyone's needs, likes, and dislikes mattered.

Now, my family members were putting their needs before mine, and I wasn't reciprocating. I was getting better and stronger, and there were some things I could do myself. But I still needed help with many tasks.

As I looked for ways to help my loved ones, I started to listen to what they needed. I forced myself to step outside of my comfortable, self-justified laziness and start trying to do the hard things I avoided (because they reminded me of my loss).

The result was quite interesting. As I focused more on others and less on myself, life became more manageable. I didn't notice the stares as much. I didn't break down to self-pitying tears quite as often. And I started noticing compassion that wasn't in me before the accident beginning to blossom.

TALKING

"And they overcame him by the blood of the Lamb, and by the word of their testimony;…" (Revelation 12:11 KJV)

I remember attending a conference where a speaker was a journalist who had been blown up by an IED in Iraq, or Afghanistan, while reporting on the war. She talked about her experience and the healing which began in the military hospital where she received treatment. Every day she was in the hospital, a psychiatrist visited her room and asked how she felt. And every day, she retold her story with a little more detail, as her brain worked to put together all the pieces and fill in the holes. She spoke honestly about her feelings.

Meanwhile, the psychiatrist also made his rounds to other patients. They were also warriors injured in battle. The psychiatrist was higher ranked than the soldiers. When he would go in and ask them how they were doing that day, their answer was always, "Fine, sir." He would then move on.

Anyone who goes through trauma experiences some level of Post-Traumatic Stress Disorder (PTSD). The way I understand PTSD is that the brain is trying to protect the body from re-experiencing trauma. The brain tries to put the pieces together, repeating the story until it fills in all the gaps.

If the person has moved away from the source of trauma, the brain can start the healing process by putting pieces together. It then tells the body it's safe from further harm; the person recovers and goes on with life. The trauma becomes part of their past.

If the trauma still exists, the brain tries to put measures in place to protect the body. This is an over-simplified explanation. The time it takes for the brain to go through this process is undetermined. For example, for a warrior returning from experiencing numerous violent events for a prolonged period of time, it can take years to unwind the trauma. In contrast, a person who witnesses a traumatic event that lasted only moments will have effects, but the time it takes for their brain to recover and deem them "safe" should, in theory, take less time.

Sometimes an environmental trigger restimulates the trauma. You may be aware of people who are stuck in their PTSD; they have significant side effects, and their past is a large part of their present life.

The journalist shared that she resumed her everyday life after leaving the hospital, experiencing minimal symptoms of PTSD. On the other hand, many of the other veterans required ongoing treatment for their mental health. An important reason this woman's brain was able to bounce back was that she talked through her trauma with the psychiatrist.

* * *

Scripture indicates part of the way we overcome is by the word of our testimony. When I speak about what is going on with me, it puts the issue in a different light. Things can circle around in my brain for quite a while; issues can get wild and distorted. When I say what I'm thinking out loud, I can see it for what it is. And I can problem-solve. I can make decisions to guide my life. Speaking these issues out loud makes them more real, bringing them into existence. It brings a measure of accountability when I share with others.

I mess up, whether by accident, mistake, misunderstanding, or not doing what I'm supposed to do. Talking about it helps me to learn from it and develop a plan not to repeat the mistake. In speaking about it, I can own up to my wrongdoing; I can help heal the wound created in someone else. Talking helps me move forward.

When I don't want to talk about an incident or circumstances in my life, it's because I feel like I'm alone, that nobody will understand what I'm going through, or that nobody can help me. There are also times I don't want to talk about something because I'm wrong. I know it, but I don't want to change. I want to hold on to whatever it is. In my life, these are typically things I feel shameful or guilty about; I think if people knew, they would reject me. Or, they are things I feel entitled to.

The temptation is to close myself off, justifying protecting myself, my emotions, or my things. The reality is, when I put my pain, entitlements, or shame in a closet—locking it away—they mutate. When I don't expose an issue to the light where others can hear it and offer their perspective, where God can forgive, it mutates. The truth becomes shaded with bitterness, lack of forgiveness, resentment, and self-pity.

The thing is, an issue never stays in the compartment I put it in; it never remains silent. It starts spilling out onto everything that touches it, sliming it. I can't leave it in the past because it's oozing into the present:

- It can hold me back from my destiny.

- It can stunt my growth.

- It can darken my relationships.

- It can alter my perception of God, of others, of myself.

- It doesn't stay silent.

- It cripples.

I believe one of the first steps to healing is talking. This action brings problems I've packed away that are stinky and moldy and stuffed in the closet into the light. It's dealing with them, sorting and analyzing them, and letting the truth shine on them.

Every time I tell my story, I heal a little more.

"Therefore confess your sins to each other and pray for each other so that you may be healed." (James 5:16 NIV)

For a long time, I thought confessing to God was enough; He's the one who forgives and heals. A level of peace did come from confession, but it limited me to what I understood. If I was brave enough to share my biggest fears, my deepest insecurities, and my most shameful thoughts to trusted, caring people who did not judge or condemn, I could start healing.

That's when I learned I wasn't alone.

COMMUNITY

At the accident scene, after exiting the car and helping Nikki out, Roseanna could only watch. She witnessed several people attempt to help, only to retreat. There was a man, unkempt, dirty, with long straggly hair, wearing a corduroy coat. He walked directly up to the car, unfazed by the heat emanating from it. He arrived by the driver's door just as I rolled out—as if he knew the moment I would be released from my seatbelt. Immediately, he wrapped me in his coat to put out the flames, then stepped back as the ambulance workers approached me.

Roseanna told me afterward that she awoke in a bed on her stomach in the emergency room. Several people came to visit. Her date, Scotty; her friend James; and his dad, Jimmy, had come to see her. Mama was by her side, trying to find a way to comfort her that wouldn't hurt. The state trooper who had held her back from the blaze walked in to check on her. She saw the scratches down his arms—the ones she had made trying to claw her way to me. The events had shaken him up, but he had done his job protecting her.

As people rotated in and out of her room, one person, in particular, stood out. It was a man, dirty and unkempt, with a corduroy coat standing quietly and peacefully at the foot of her bed, smiling at her. He went unnoticed by everyone else that evening, but Roseanna knew he had been in the right place at the right time; could he have been an angel?

"Carry each other's burdens, and in this way you will fulfill the law of Christ." (Galatians 6:2 NIV)

The paramedics, state trooper, firefighters, ambulance personnel, emergency room nurses and doctors, helicopter pilots, life jet nurses, the burn care team, therapists, psychologists, and counselors were only some of the people involved in saving our lives. The home health nurses, personal care assistants, administrative staff, custodial staff, transportation services, fundraisers, and volunteers all played a significant part in helping two teenage girls have their best chance at life.

Additionally, we had the tremendous support of family, friends, churches, teachers, employers, and community members. That's just the beginning. The support went on for years, across states, in all the stages of healing. There have been countless prayers, reassuring smiles, unconditional love, encouraging words, hard truths, and probing questions that have come from loved ones, trusted professionals, and kind strangers. These have come on the darkest days as well as those most celebrated.

It's astounding the number of people who have touched my life—those who sacrificed their days, nights, comfort, and time with their loved ones for my well-being. It's humbling.

They have been a constant all along the way—when

- it feels I can't take another step.

- confusion clouds the path.

- the pain seems unbearable.

- there are more questions than answers.

- I forget whose I am.

- I feel the weakest.

- the lies swarm around me.

I have the gift of a community—a mass of people who have played a role in my healing. Together, they combat the lie that I am all alone; nobody understands me. To believe nobody can help me isolates me from the thing I need the most—community—and leaves me feeling hopeless.

Those around me remind me every day that the struggle is for more than myself, and there is always victory on the other side of pain. One of the hardest things I had to do was receive gifts from others I can never pay back. Therein lies the healing; I can never achieve it alone. God created us to be part of a family, a community, a body of people.

> THOSE AROUND ME REMIND ME EVERY DAY THAT THE STRUGGLE IS FOR MORE THAN MYSELF, AND THERE IS ALWAYS VICTORY ON THE OTHER SIDE OF PAIN.

Just as healing has come from talking, freedom has come from taking my place in the community around me:

- I get to listen to others' challenges.

- I get to belong.

- I hear their fears and voice my own.

- I learn from them.

- We grow together.

- I get to contribute to their lives, feel like my life has meaning, and see that it's not all about me.

There is incredible value—a life-cycle of giving, receiving, loving, and being loved—that instills purpose and facilitates healthy growth. It's bigger than me.

When someone reaches out

- to hug me,

- to remind me I am loved,

- to speak a blessing over my life,

- to tell me I am beautiful, have a purpose, and not forgotten,

it's as if, for a moment, I get to feel God's arms around me. I can hear His audible voice and know His will. The distance between God and me closes, the clouds part, and my view of life becomes a little clearer.

"Just as our bodies have many parts and each part has a special function, so it is with Christ's body. We are many parts of one body, and we all belong to each other.

In his grace, God has given us different gifts for doing certain things well. So if God has given you the ability to prophesy, speak out with as much faith as God has given you. If your gift is serving others, serve them well. If you are a teacher, teach well. If your gift is to encourage others, be encouraging. If it is giving, give generously. If God has given you leadership ability, take the responsibility seriously. And if you have a gift for showing kindness to others, do it gladly.

Don't just pretend to love others. Really love them. Hate what is wrong. Hold tightly to what is good. Love each other with genuine affection, and take delight in honoring each other."
(Romans 12:4-10)

It's important to note that when I've been

- prideful and thinking I can handle it all on my own, or nobody can help me;

- filled with guilt and shame and believing if others only knew the truth, they would discard me;

- filled with unbelief and feeling God's promises are true for others, but not me;

- forgetful of my value and who I am with Christ in me;

I genuinely feel alone; I feel detached and lost as if I'm aimlessly floating in the ocean with no view of the shore. My hope begins to dwindle, and my problems outweigh my faith. When I push past my fear of rejection and being alone, when I close my ears to their taunts, I choose to be

- transparent,
- vulnerable,

- and accountable, and

- then I can heal effectively.

I thought so many things were "normal," only to discover they are simply "my normal." Beliefs I developed in the confines of how my family operated and my parents trained me produced the way I translated the world around me. So, there were things I dealt with and faced that weren't always necessary. Sometimes, I made finding a solution harder than it needed to be because I wasn't aware of another way to deal with it.

People who have peace and joy in their lives can show me another way of approaching life. In being transparent and vulnerable with trusted people, I learned to express what I wanted. With fresh eyes, others can sometimes see the self-defense and self-preservation I've put in place. These are things I don't know about myself that get in the way of healing.

In love, these people can point out to me the self-destructive mindsets holding me back. They can join with me in prayer and invite the freedom given by Christ into my situation. Remaining accountable—leaving an open line of communication about my struggles—means when unhealthy ways of thinking or destructive patterns try to re-emerge, I can nip them in the bud before they have grown to entangle and imprison me.

It's crazy; the most challenging and scariest thing to do—being transparent and vulnerable—can be the pathway to freedom. *How often do I have to actually walk into my biggest fears to be freed of them?*

"How good and pleasant it is when God's people live together in unity! . . . For For there the LORD *bestows his blessing, even life forevermore." (Psalm 133:1, 3 NIV)*

4

GRIEVING LOSSES

"You keep track of all my sorrows. You have collected all my tears in Your bottle. You have recorded each one in Your book." (Psalm 56:8 NLT)

I'm a girl—we cry. I don't like that fact about myself. It's always been messy, inconvenient, and out of my control. Sometimes emotion builds slowly over time; other times, the tears are determined to fall no matter where I am, what I'm doing, or who I'm with. They come when I'm confused, overwhelmed, or over-tired. They come when I'm angry, hurt, insecure, scared, or even brave. There are times they come from the depths of my soul in worship or gratitude and joy.

After the accident, my tears flowed freely, especially the first year, as I adjusted to my changed face and body, my life without fingers, and to my weaknesses and inabilities. They came from

- the pain of dressing changes, therapy, and surgeries;

- the frustration of re-learning how to do simple things that once came so naturally;

- altered life plans;

- others telling me what I couldn't do, what I would never be able to do; or

- limiting me to their perception of me and my life.

But I was still thankful:

- No one died in the accident.

- I didn't lose all my fingers.

- I didn't lose a limb.

- I still had some vision.

- There was enough skin to repair.

I concluded I didn't suffer loss, so there was nothing to grieve. In my seventeen-year-old mind, death caused grief; it didn't occur to me that we grieve for other reasons.

Several years later—after many surgeries, adjusting to my new body, and stepping out on my own to prove to everyone that the scars would not define me—a good friend suggested I needed to grieve my loss. It was a gaping emotional wound that I hadn't acknowledged but needed to heal. This was an eye-opener to me.

There are many losses we have in life we do not grieve because

- they don't involve loss of life—therefore, the loss was not big enough—we should be thankful instead;

- we don't feel it's important enough to grieve;

- we don't feel important enough to be given time and space to grieve;

- we do not know how to grieve;

- it's messy;

- we don't know what to do around others who are grieving;

- grieving hurts—who wants to put themselves through hurt?

Allowing any of those excuses to keep me from grieving caused me to get stuck. I kept reliving the pain of loss but tried to ignore it. Or I told myself it was wrong to feel that way. By not genuinely grieving my losses, I couldn't move forward.

For me, the losses I had to acknowledge were significant, authentic, and worth grieving.

LOSSES

> The loss of my face
> > my beauty,
> > my identity,
> > > who I knew myself to be.
> The loss of my fingers
> > lost functionality,
> > the previous ease with which I was
> > > able to create things,
> > > untie tricky knots,
> > > put the backs on my earrings.
> The loss of my skin
> > smooth and beautiful,
> > regulating my body temperature,
> > aging at a normal rate.
> > Now wrinkled and discolored.
> The loss of my hair
> > thick and luscious,
> > wash and go style.
> The loss of plans
> > my plans
> > > for the future.

The loss of normalness
    others considering me as normal,
    others seeing me and
        not staring,
        or judging,
        or determining who I was
            without getting to know me.
The reality
    these scars
        something I will carry forever,
        forever bringing me a challenge
        of some sort or another.

* * *

Once I voiced these sorrows, they didn't seem to pop up in my everyday life. The loss inside of me was acknowledged and no longer screaming to be known. I had unwittingly been trying to silence recognition of my grief which was required to heal.

When I'm frustrated or challenged by one of those losses, I can quickly validate my emotion and move forward—instead of burying it, letting it fester and demand to be heard in ugly ways—ways that affect me and those closest to me.

Now, I'm learning another type of grief—losing people I love. The anguish of no longer being able to reach them, see them, or hold them comes in waves as I create a new future without them in it.

Grief doesn't cycle. You don't go through each stage once and overcome it. Grief comes in waves. I can feel all the phases at once, then not at all. Then, another wave of pain comes crashing down when I least expect it, taking my breath away, sweeping my feet out from under me. Other times, small waves lap at my ankles, reminders, sweet memories, gentle nudges.

Life changes, fulfilling long-desired promises, and making new dreams. I move forward into the unknown. It's essential to voice even the grief that comes in celebrations and follows unfulfilled expectations, broken promises, and false hopes. Otherwise, suffering becomes a festering wound, filled with bitterness and resentment, robbing me of joy, replacing my gratitude, and poisoning my path.

Grief isn't supposed to consume me all the time. Loss is not my present or my future. The past and all it held—the trauma and pain—is past; I don't need to make it a daily part of my present. It's valid, genuine, and can be processed and dealt with when it comes up. However, there comes the point when, in dealing with the past, I'm not living in today.

Where does my help come from? It comes from the Lord—the One who made the mountains and a way over those mountains. The One who made me and knows how I encounter obstacles, the strength I have, and the muscle I need to build—the One who knows what is on the other side and what's along the way.

"...I lift up my eyes up to the mountains—where does my help come from? My help comes from the LORD, the maker of heaven and earth." (Psalm 121:1-2 NIV)

The mountains can be a symbol of grandeur, majestic beauty, and great heights; they can also be overwhelming obstacles, much larger than myself, with no apparent, easy path over them. To scale and overcome requires a lot of time, energy, and devotion. These mountains might represent jobs, marriages, relationships, traumas, and other life changes.

A life's journey has sections with no pathway, where one is walking in the dark, stumbling up hills, carrying a huge weight, one foot in front of the other. It can take every bit of effort to stay upright and keep moving forward at those moments when I can't see my surroundings. Sometimes I need to stop and process

- where I am,
- where I have been,

- where I am going,

- how far along I am in the journey,

- what the end will look like,

- or how I got there in the first place.

Maybe there are parts of the journey that I don't need to process. Perhaps I only need to get through those. I am the only one who can move myself forward—others can walk beside me here and there along the way, but they can't complete the course on my behalf. Others can't take the weight of life from me; they can't fix me. The majority of the journey—day after day, week after week, month after month—is mine to walk alone. Yet, I'm never truly alone.

> *"God is our refuge and strength, an ever-present help in trouble. Therefore we will not fear, though the earth give way and the mountains fall into the heart of the sea, though its waters roar and foam and the mountains quake with their surging."*
> *(Psalm 46:1-3 NIV)*

PAIN

When people see me, one of the first things they say is, "Whoa!" I know because some people speak before they think when they come across my path. They usually follow up with, "She's been through a lot."

Anybody who has endured burns can identify with this injury because they know it hurts. Those who are empathetic recall the pain they felt when their hand bore the mark of coming into contact with a hot object. They try to imagine that same pain over 75 percent of their body.

When I was injured, I experienced pain I could not escape from; it wasn't fleeting; it wasn't short-lived. It was excruciating pain, inflicted over and over for long periods, with no escape or reprieve, a constant cycle of pain and pain management.

My younger sister was also healing from burns on 30 percent of her body. I lived with the knowledge that my mistake caused her great pain and resulted in her spending a month in the hospital, forced to bear scars for the rest of her life. Scars result from injury and can be unnoticeable, as my sister's are, or plainly visible, like mine.

While I was in the children's hospital, I experienced something to distract me from my pain. It was the awareness that inside the other hospital rooms, there were younger children who all had their own stories of pain, each with their own family struggling to cope.

The children might not have seen the tears I saw when I looked into the eyes of the dedicated staff as they performed their duties and listened to our screams. From time to time, I heard stories about some of the children. Their injuries weren't accidents; people caused them who were supposed to protect them. Somehow, this altered my perspective.

My accident didn't kill me, and it wasn't intentional. No one hurt me; the fire did. My burns did get better, and there was less pain over time. I had only the work of healing. Children injured as punishment have a scope of suffering I've never experienced.

When I am in great pain, it is effortless for my world to become very small. It becomes all about me. In this horrible situation, many factors in my life kept me from focusing on myself for too long. I wasn't the only one who was hurt. I also had people who cared about me besides my family, doing difficult things for me, like my wound care.

Had I sought to escape the pain and refused these miserable ordeals, infection would have set in. I would have become immobilized or even died. People who could see farther ahead than me, knowledgeable people with great inner strength, had inflicted the necessary pain to save my life.

The agony established a threshold in my life, though. Now I knew how much I could tolerate. Because it was way more than the average aches and pain, I have also learned that I can endure a lot without fear. I know where my boundary lines are, and I often walk right up to them, refusing to let them limit me anymore. Sometimes my family members don't like this very much.

This new approach to my limits applies to emotional and spiritual growth as well. When I try to avoid pain, trials, or discomfort, I allow my fear of being hurt or my fear of the unknown to stunt my growth. But pain does not last forever, even when we think it might. On the other side of the distress is victory and strength, qualities which would be unattainable if I circumvented my discomfort.

Does that mean I like pain? Not at all; I enjoy a life full of happiness, and I'm content.

When problems come, I've learned that the best way to deal with them is to walk straight into them. The longer I try to deny the presence of pain or to avoid its grasp, the longer it takes for me to see the treasure waiting on the other side. And there always is a reward.

I often get the courage to face pain by remembering how I've made it through much worse. I remember the truth of how brave I am when I don't feel courageous at all. As I recall the truth of who I am and how much I am loved, and as I choose to believe this truth, pain no longer rules me. It becomes my servant and a stepping stone to overcoming it.

When I don't learn from or avoid the lessons of my trials or demean my tribulations, then perseverance, endurance, character, and hope don't have room to grow in my life.

"And not only that, but we also glory in tribulations, knowing that tribulation produces perseverance; and perseverance, character; and character, hope. Now hope does not disappoint,

because the love of God has been poured out in our hearts by the Holy Spirit who was given to us." (Romans 5:3-5)

* * *

Flames licked my skin, leaving their permanent mark for the world to see. When people see me, some are moved to compassion and kindness. They excuse my weaknesses and make room for my shortcomings. Others have difficulty seeing past the scars to my humanity. They may think less or more of me than I am for my experience. I'm a young woman with a personality, strengths, weaknesses, joys, and sorrows, just like anyone else.

For countless people without visible wounds but who suffer emotional injuries, it's as if lava was poured down their throats, mangling their insides, leaving them in anguish. They are walking around with scars hidden from sight. Because the wounds aren't seen, they are not nurtured. As the injury goes untreated, infection takes its hold, distorting truth, festering lies, and permanently changing the person's identity.

Without the ability to recognize the internal war zones others carry, one often feels alone and hopeless. We continuously trigger landmines, causing further desolation. When I have a deep wound—whether the source is unknown, infected, and painful or known, cleaned up, stitched up, and healing—there's a time when both the wound and everything that comes into its vicinity hurts. Moving hurts, laughing hurts, the ordinary things in life hurt. Those symptoms repeatedly point to problems we can address.

When the source of a wound is identified, a treatment plan must be made and implemented. This intervention, in itself, can cause pain. Then, there's the healing process, which requires facing the pain, which will subside over time. Eventually, that pain may no longer be there at all. The only thing that remains might be a scar, a reminder of the trauma that was once there.

When I don't acknowledge that a wound exists or determine it doesn't need treatment, then the symptomatic cycle will continue. Everything that comes close to the actual injury will hurt, with no hope of diminishing the pain. The rest of the body will start compensating, possibly denying the distress by building a wall around it or perhaps blaming it on other things.

I can place defense mechanisms around it, so nothing touches that spot in an attempt to minimize the effects. The result decreases my quality of life and relationships and increases the risks I take. It creates new discomfort; it results in those around me catering and bowing to my trauma; it becomes the center of everything.

If the pain is emanating from an unknown source, I begin trouble-shooting. It hurts when I do this, when I'm touched there, or when I move this way. I can analyze the timing, the side effects, and pain levels and draw a conclusion. At this point, I've likely identified the source and can develop a corresponding treatment plan. I might carry out my idea, only to discover I misdiagnosed the problem.

If I treated something bumping the wound instead of the injury itself—like cutting a weed instead of pulling it from the root, I had to troubleshoot again. I try to remember, along the way, the pain itself is not the enemy. It's an indicator that something is broken or healing.

I believe that God, in His kindness, allows people or circumstances to come into my life and bump their hidden wounds so that they can identify their trouble and seek healing.

When someone comes along and touches the button (wound) but seems to press it repeatedly, holding it down or laying on it like a car horn, it's easy to blame the person—assuming they are the source of the pain. When, in reality, that person is only the one who has gotten close to the boo-boo. The wound may have been there for a long time, lying dormant, unable to alert me to its presence as I continually distract myself from anything resembling discontent in my current circumstances.

But God allows the pain to surface so He can bring healing. He knows the deep-seated wounds I may not even know. He sees the coping mechanisms I have put into place to protect myself. God observes the walls I've built around those spots, the weapons I have taken up to arm myself against future invasion. He hears the lies that I've sown into my perceptions of others and the world around me. He notices the ways I have built my life around those lies:

- the broken mindsets I call "normal;"

- the habits I have justified;

- the promises and vows I have made to myself and others that start with the words "I will, I will not, I will never, I will always…"

He aches at the limitations I set simply because of an unhealed wound. My self-preservation takes the throne, pushing away the Healer until unbelief settles in. My perception of myself, of what I will do, what I can do, how far I can go, or what others think of me, becomes the idol to whom I bow. Instead of trusting God and believing what He, a being who cannot lie, says about me, I reject His offer of solace.

That limited self-perception then becomes the wound, a wound caused by the enemy of our souls. The enemy who:

- came to steal, kill, and destroy.

- would like nothing better than to separate me from the God who loves me.

- attempts to convince me I have no purpose, destiny, victory, or future.

- wants me to live a life of no importance, responsibility, or authority.

That wound, left undiagnosed and untreated, can be the very thing holding me back from living my destiny, purpose, and calling. It restrains me from living the limitless life given to me through Christ Jesus, from seeing miracles, and observing freedom in my life and the lives of others. All this is because I don't want to walk through the pain of healing. But God is a perfect Father, absolute love, and not afraid of allowing pain into my life.

The heavenly Father who created me knows my innermost being, yet called me His very own. God calls me by name and makes me joint-heirs with Christ—meaning I inherit His kingdom. The One who put the same spirit and power that raised Christ from the dead inside of me trusted me with it. God loves me with an everlasting love that does not change or grow when I succeed or diminish when I mess up. He provided a way I could be saved, forgiven—not just once—but repeatedly.

Often I find myself hurting—my heart wanting something I don't have, can't see, or have waited for a long time. I find myself coming up on another holiday season, a new year, or another birthday. I have a few quiet moments when life isn't hectic, and my mind isn't focused on the "to do" list or the needs of my loved ones. During those moments when I'm thinking about me and my lack, I ask God, "This year, Lord, can it be this year You fulfill that desire of my heart?" I discover tears slipping down my cheeks. I find myself telling Him how many years I've been hoping, praying, waiting, and asking, but not receiving. I inform Him it hurts to continue patiently.

> GOD LOVES ME WITH AN EVERLASTING LOVE THAT DOES NOT CHANGE OR GROW WHEN I SUCCEED OR DIMINISH WHEN I MESS UP.

The goal of displacing my pain is not what compels Him to move on my behalf and fulfill His promise. He sees farther than my temporary distress, but my suffering will not deter Him as He isn't afraid of it. Jesus' pain—being pulverized and executed on our behalf—did not cause the Father to run to His rescue because it would have left the work incomplete. His agony would have been for nothing.

God is faithful. He allows suffering to remain in my life until its purpose is complete, so it is not wasted. This doesn't mean the Lord delights in seeing me hurt. Nor does it mean He goes to another room and covers His ears where He can't see or hear my cries until the appointed time.

He sent the Holy Spirit as my comforter because He knew there would be times in life when I needed comfort and reminders.

- The joy set before Christ spurred Him onward to endure the cross and the shame heaped upon Him.

- He, too, wept with those who mourned.

- While I hurt, God will never leave me or forsake me—even though I can't see the path ahead or why His promises are taking so long to be fulfilled.

- I don't need to be afraid to voice the deep desires of my heart to Him.

- I'm blessed, even though I sometimes think about what I lack.

- It's my privilege to knock and keep knocking.

God is not displeased with me and withholding good things from me as a result. He doesn't play games with me. When I acknowledge the sacrifice Jesus made on my behalf and receive His gift—which came at an unconscionable cost—then all Father sees in me is His daughter—with whom He is well pleased. This fact doesn't change. He doesn't change.

I believe God sees pain as a temporary problem in an eternal life. He is much more concerned with my character than my brief discomfort.

I get to choose if I trust and agree with Him. When I do, the grace to endure is improved, and the pain seems to subside.

5

FAITH

Throughout our childhood, Mama told us this story. "I was six years old, and your granny had been dating grandpa for a while. He was a tall, strong, handsome army man with a generous heart, and granny worked at the army base.

"When he wanted to marry her, he came to me first and asked me, 'I would like to marry your mom. Can I be your daddy?' Of course, I said, 'Yes!'

"A few months later, Daddy came to pick me up from school. He was skipping, jumping, whooping, and hollering down the hall. He came up to me and excitedly showed me the papers he had in his hand. 'I was able to adopt you! I am so excited to be your daddy!' We held hands and skipped down the hallway together as we exited the building.

"I often picture that day and think of our Heavenly Father and His pure joy when we invite him into our lives. This is what a father's heart is."

As a child, I believed. It was a simple faith based on love—safe, kind, love in its innocent form. Jesus was a Son, and His Father was a perfect Father. I learned the language and memorized the verse:

"For God so loved the world that He gave His one and only Son, that whoever believes in Him shall not perish but have eternal life." (John 3:16 NIV)

I tried to be good. As I grew, I began to understand "right and wrong," "good and bad." There were consequences to my bad choices, and I hated them. So, being "good" became a necessity to avoid discipline. My inner struggle began.

It was a challenge to do the right thing, especially if I didn't feel like it. It was also a fight not to get caught when I indulged myself, like when I said mean things to my sisters or disobeyed my parents.

I struggled to be a good Christian, pray, and read my Bible, even if I didn't understand it. I believed that if I did things "right," I would be accepted and loved unconditionally. But if I didn't, I would be excommunicated from longed-for acceptance.

Deep inside, I loved God the best I knew how; I stood up for Him, and some misunderstood or made fun of me because of this. Silence became a shield to hide behind. I was "Charity Church-mouse."

By the time I was a teenager, my struggles had turned inward. I rarely received discipline because I became my own taskmaster—observing others and creating a list of rules to follow, so I would not be noticed, embarrassed, made fun of, or perceived as different.

Anytime I did something to merit negative attention, I rebuked myself heavily—vowing not to repeat the action. When I did something resulting in discipline, I got much angrier than my parents—making myself judge, jury, and executioner. By the time I was sixteen, my list of dos and don'ts was very long, and I was weary of feeling naïve and embarrassed. I decided that since the Bible was written over 2,000 years ago, its rules couldn't apply to today's scenarios.

I walked away from my faith to find answers to my questions on my own.

I was quiet, shy, and insecure. Like most teenagers, I *hoped* I would do great things in my life—like be an outstanding artist or the perfect wife and mother—but honestly, I just tried to make good choices and ensure nobody disliked me. I thought that was the key to living "happily ever after."

I'd like to say my brush with death gave me incredible faith, this "knowing" about God and His goodness, and gratitude to be alive. But that's not the case. A couple of months before the accident, I did recommit my life to God. I asked for His forgiveness because I had chosen to go my own way instead of obeying Him. My way caused me to be selfish and hurt the people I loved. It was foolish and was leading to undesired consequences. My path was full of lies and deceptions and the guilt that came from them.

So, I went back to the One I knew had good plans for my life, who loved me, and who would protect and care for me. I walked in faith; it was small, but a seed, nonetheless. I wanted to believe that God is good and His ways were better than my ways.

* * *

At the age of seventeen, I thought I was a wimp. I had never been hurt or sick enough to go to the hospital. There were a couple of times I had hurt myself. At school, I once hit my funny bone hard and passed out!

When the accident happened, prayer immediately surrounded us. My mama sat by my bed, singing, praying, reading the Bible, and playing music. It was like church all day, every day. It was good.

I needed the constant reminder that God was on my side. Somehow my little bit of faith sprouted while I waited through my pain. Maybe it was because the accident was my fault, perhaps because I knew it was me who hit the brakes, causing the car to spin out of control. Somehow, I knew this injury, this horrible suffering, wasn't His doing. I couldn't blame Him.

What I did understand, I heard from the doctors. This battle was a big deal, and recovery would take a long time. I wasn't going to be all better one day—as if it never happened. There would always be scars and limitations. When I began to grasp the severity of it all, I knew I needed something much bigger than me to help me through it. I knew God was my Savior, not my enemy.

He, my Creator, My Heavenly Father, knew so much before I was ever born. He knew

- the family I would be given to—their strengths and their weaknesses;

- how they would receive the news of my arrival;

- which family traits He wanted me to have;

- what order I should be in my family unit;

- all the gifts and talents I would possess;

- the personality that would best serve me;

- what my favorite things would be;

- the things that would bring me great joy and delight, amusement, and encouragement;

- where I would be weak and what traits would challenge me;

- He would choose me, and I would choose Him;

- the measure of faith He had given me.

He knew all this before I was ever born. None of this was hard for Him because He gave me a measure of what brings Him joy.

He also knew the hardships I would face. Troubles are common to the human race.

Some difficulties are because we live on Earth and must abide by the planet's laws of nature; some result from our choices and their consequences, and others occur because of selfishness and humans inflicting their wills upon others.

Sometimes it all collides into a tragedy. Unexpected trials carry significant loss, requiring more faith and strength than we think we have, to go on with the business of living the journey that God allotted to us.

He knew when He created me that I would need a measure of tenacity and resolve. Thus, a pragmatic yet sensitive approach to life would benefit me. Faith would be essential, transparency would serve me well, and love would be my anchor.

I believe God wept as He foresaw the pain I would endure as He has seen so many go through the unthinkable. But Heavenly Father also sees beyond the pain to what will occur.

So, God wove into me gifts I would not recognize until I needed them. He set me on a course that would prepare me for life. When I consider that God, as my creator and Father, was working on my behalf to give me a hopeful future before I was ever born, how can I feel anything but adoration for Him? And that's not even the beginning of all He is.

* * *

The Bible says if I have faith the size of a mustard seed, then I can say to that mountain, "Move," and it will move. When we commit our lives to Jesus, we plant a seed of eternal faith inside us. We can water that seed and let it grow, or we can hide it away where it will lie dormant until given the attention it needs. Watering that seed happens through prayer, reading the Word, and walking in obedience. His life-giving power

LIFE BEYOND THE SCARS

allows that sprout to grow. The fascinating thing is, many times, we don't know how big or how healthy our faith is until we encounter trials.

When I was twenty-five, my doctor had known me for seven years, and I remember him saying, "Charity, the biggest thing that stands out about you is your faith; please don't lose that."

I remember thinking, *Is my faith really noticeable? Yes, I believe in God; I love Him; I know He's the only one who can help us through the most challenging times of life. When I think of people with great faith, I think of pastors and teachers who know the Bible inside and out and those who pray for others and see them healed. People with active faith go to other countries and endure significant discomfort to tell the lost about Jesus. I'm just a typical young adult with fears and insecurities, and I wonder what I'm supposed to do with my life. I don't have all the answers; I hope when I'm old, I can look back on my life and see it's made a difference to somebody.*

Some events come along in life that test us. I think the tests are more for our sakes than God's sake, so we can begin to know who we are, what we'll do when the rubber meets the road. God already knows. We *hope* we'll respond well when life gets tough, we *imagine* we'll say or do the right thing, but we don't really *know*.

Then my test came.

How are you *supposed* to react when you discover the largest organ of your body—its primary defense layer against disease and infection, your skin—has been permanently damaged?

How was *I*, a seventeen-year-old, supposed to respond when they told me I'd have a ten percent chance of living, and if I did live, I would have to endure countless surgeries?

How was I supposed to respond when I discovered my younger sister, one of my best friends, is in the next room in excruciating pain with her beautiful red hair shaved off because *I* was driving that night?

How was I supposed to respond when they told me, an aspiring artist, that I would probably lose my right fingers unless a miracle happened? I heard the information, and I took it in, and my response was—we'll adjust; we'll make it through. This must be faith, the substance of things hoped for, the evidence of things not yet seen.

The peace that was deep down wasn't something I could make happen; it must have been a byproduct of believing in a God who is too huge to see and asking Jesus into your heart.

My inclination not to react, but to take in the information and look for hope, must be the way God created me or the measure of faith He gave me. It must be the result of all those who prayed.

Faith was evident in my pregnant mother's prayers, who sat by my bed, singing to me, reading to me, and speaking life over me. Faith pleases God; He loves it when we entrust Him with our circumstances. It also takes the pressure off of us to fix things that are way too much for us.

Jesus had faith before he started His ministry and before He did any miracles—other than solving the catering dilemma—before He raised the dead, opened blind eyes, healed withered hands, or straightened crooked backs, before he "accomplished" anything. Upon the public declaration of His faith and absolute surrender to the Father through water baptism—the Father publicly declared, "This is my beloved Son in whom I am well pleased."

"And without faith, it is impossible to please God, because anyone who comes to him must believe that he exists and that he rewards those who earnestly seek him." (Hebrews 11:6 NIV)

With faith, that tiny seed of faith, is it possible this is all that's required to please God? Maybe it gives Him the ingredient necessary to do the impossible.

"…not by might, nor by power, but by My Spirit says the LORD *Almighty." (Zechariah 4:6 NIV)*

That same Spirit who raised Christ from the dead dwells in me. So, maybe it's not about how much I get or understand. Perhaps it's about my seed of faith and putting it into God's hands to do what only He can do. Recognizing my works aren't what leads to His favor, but rather it's my faith that gives me favor.

"I pray that out of His glorious riches He may strengthen you with power through His Spirit in your inner being, so that Christ may dwell in your hearts through faith. And I pray that you, being rooted and established in love, may have power, together with all the Lord's holy people, to grasp how wide and long and high and deep is the love of Christ, and to know this love that surpasses knowledge—that you may be filled to the measure of all the fullness of God. Now to Him who is able to do immeasurably more than all we ask or imagine, according to His power that is at work within us, to Him be glory…" (Ephesians 3:16-21 NIV)

The reality strikes me that faith has a lot more power than we give it credit for. If some trust and hope can allow us to be "filled to the measure of all the fullness of God," then there is truly nothing we cannot accomplish. It is a very humbling notion that God would be willing to fill us and to trust us with His power.

I think of how often my faith, my greatest prayers, and the way I imagine they will be or could be answered is so small. It's limited to my narrow scope of life and the little I have experienced or read. He tells us He'll do "immeasurably more than all we ask or imagine…". He wants to; that's where the depth of His love for us comes into play.

Lately, I've been witnessing God working in people's lives, moving mountains, changing directions, granting favor, and blessing them. It all playing out differently than I would ever have thought for them when I offered up prayers on their behalf. I'm left wondering, *how much am I missing?* How often do I limit faith to an attitude, when in reality I am squelching its power with my traditional mindsets?

MIRACLES

I was eighteen months old. Still not walking or crawling, I rolled wherever I wanted to go. The doctors told my mama, "Your daughter has a problem with her hips; we can't define it. She's not using them at all; be prepared—she may never be able to walk."

Mama never voiced the words the doctors spoke; instead, she took them to God.

One day Mama was at church. She carried me as she made her way out the door a woman (now known to us as Aunt Betsy) approached her. "Can I pray for your daughter?"

"Yes, I would like that," Mama said.

"What's her name?"

"Her name is Charity."

The lady put her hands on my little head and prayed, "Father God, I pray that you would bless Charity. I pray You would strengthen her little legs, help her to grow strong, and always know Your love for her."

"Thank you for praying; you have no idea how much we needed that prayer."

A couple of weeks later, we were back at church. I was in the care of the church nursery. They had me outside, and I didn't want to roll in the prickly grass. So, I stood up and walked.

My life has portrayed miracles big and small from the beginning, with the first being my birth. My mother had a miscarriage a couple of months before my conception, and I've lived with the knowledge that, had that baby lived, I wouldn't exist. These examples followed me through my childhood.

* * *

I often think of Jesus, His time on Earth, the miracles He performed. Many of them seemed to result from people's faith—the woman with the issue of blood, the father whose son had a deaf and dumb spirit, the Centurion whose servant Jesus healed by a word, the man let down through the rafters of the roof, brought to Jesus by his friends. The stories go on and on. A man stretches out a shriveled hand, another washes mud from his eyes, and one picks up his mat and walks.

These people didn't have to be Bible scholars to be healed. They didn't have to fast and pray or come up with the right words. Jesus didn't play games with them or require proof of salvation before moving with compassion and mercy on their behalf.

They came to Him. He saw a need, and He had answers. In their moment of trial, they agreed with Him enough:

- to stretch out a hand,

- to wash out their eyes,

- to pick up their mat,

- to confess their unbelief.

The faith of a mustard seed was enough, and the miracles reinforced and grew their faith. Faith and miracles go hand-in-hand. In the life of Jesus, they are inseparable. He met each person in their weakness. He took the measure of faith they had—whatever size it was—and He completed it with His own, presenting the full extent and providing the entire request.

It's kind of like an adult taking the change of a small child and adding their dollars to it to complete a purchase. One wouldn't expect a child with no means of income to provide for their own needs and wants. But one can accept what little a child can offer freely, know her heart's intention, and make sure the child is well cared for, simply because the child is their own and she is loved.

I wonder how often I make miracles out to be much more complicated and deem them much more impossible than they really are. When in reality, they are all around me, intricately mixed with my faith, accessible to me at all times, and happening without my awareness. All I need to do is open my eyes to see them.

* * *

We sat in the blue 1966 Falcon, parked in front of Madison Park, eating lunch consisting of Popeye's Chicken. It was a chilly January day. Clay was in the back, strapped into his car seat.

"I think I may be pregnant," Mama stated.

I responded, "Oh, that's so exciting! Clay needs a little brother or sister. That will be good for him to have someone to play with! Do you know how far along you are?"

"If I am pregnant, it would just be a couple of weeks."

"Have you thought about names?" I asked.

"I don't know about boy names yet, but if it's a girl, I've always liked the name Laura Rose. Laura means victory, and I love the name Rose—but it's very similar to Roseanna's name, so I think we'll have to come up with a different middle name. I still have to tell your Papa. And there are risks considering my age."

She was correct; pregnancy at forty years old was considered high risk. However, we had to have faith that it would be all right.

* * *

She spent her first trimester in the hospital at the bedsides of Roseanna and me. The nurses watched over Mama and protected her and her unborn baby from news that might shock her (like me dying and them having to resuscitate me while my dad watched from my sister's room).

Despite the circumstances, my mother went full-term and had a perfect baby girl, Laura Sue, a miracle. I often think how easily one car accident could have taken three daughters from my mother that night. The laughter and joy Laura brought to our lives on the tail end of tragedy have been a gift beyond words.

There were other miracles too.

When my seatbelt snapped immediately after uttering the words, "It needs to be cut, or burnt through…" I knew it was an angel who cut my seatbelt. This detail was reinforced in me more when I realized seat belts don't burn through; the nylon material melts and hardens. Furthermore, the buckle itself was found still intact in the wreckage.

There was no flight visibility the night of the accident. The storm had grounded all aircraft. Yet, we needed to be flown by helicopter out to the nearest burn hospital. The skies opened up just long enough to allow us to be transported.

After being in the burn hospital for five days, where they waited to see if I'd survive before starting any surgeries, Shriners Hospital for Children invited us for treatment. Once we were life-flighted there, they immediately commenced a life-saving operation, the first of six to be done in the next two and a half months.

All of our treatment was at no cost to our family.

The majority of my surgeries went much better than imagined.

I was released from the hospital after two and a half months. They thought the release was temporary and that I'd be re-admitted within a couple of weeks, but I did better than expected.

I healed and regained strength and range of motion quicker than most—although a year of therapy and complete dependency didn't seem quick to me at all.

My plastic surgeon happened to be hired on at Shriners just as I was starting my reconstructive surgeries. He had a more modern approach to reconstructive surgeries, including the timeline they usually happened on. This expertise allowed me to have operations that helped me gain function and feel a little bit more "normal" in appearance. It felt like he was sent there just for me.

These were only some of the miracles that happened during that time. They were reminders that God was real, He was on our side, and He was taking care of us.

"You are a miracle!" I've heard this exclamation dozens of times. It's true, and I'm thankful. I'm alive, sane, and making healthy life choices. Also, I'm not bitter, angry, or limited. All of this is truly miraculous. I have steady, loving relationships; I can walk in security and confidence, knowing who I am and whose I am; those are miracles.

These things have been given to me, not because I earned them, deserve them, or prayed the proper petitions, but because God is faithful and kind. He is a miracle-working God who made way for us to be in the right relationship with Him. Through the death of His Son, the perfect sacrifice, we receive blessings of forgiveness and grace. When I simply believe He is who He says He is, and when I receive His gift, I am accepting the miracle of His sacrifice.

The act of faith is miraculous, and miracles are the result of faith, so interwoven, they cannot be separated from each other.

Along the way, we've prayed for the impossible. Many people have joined their faith to mine. We've stretched our hearts to the brink of our understanding, pushed past what we can see, reached into the realm of the unseen, grabbed onto the greater truths, and tried to hold them for ourselves. We've prayed with fervor and expectancy, dispelled unbelief, and claimed all that Christ Jesus gave us through His complete gift on the cross. We've asked for, proclaimed, and declared complete healing for my body.

Visions of smoothed scars and fingers growing back have filled the hearts of many brave prayer warriors who stepped up and asked me if they too could pray for the miraculous.

I once heard a teaching about intercession. The speaker was referring to the story of the widow in Luke 18. The latter approached the judge repeatedly until he finally conceded to giving her justice so she would stop bothering him.

The speaker referred to our intercession as being akin to chopping down a tree. Some trees are gigantic and formidable; you can give blow after blow with an ax, and it seems as if you are not getting anywhere at all. However, if you keep going, there will eventually be a blow that causes the tree to topple.

When it comes to praying for miracles in my life—for my healing—I've found the safest place is in God's hands. I recognize my very existence is a miracle. Then there's the miraculous work done on the cross for my salvation—for my life-changing relationship with God. The Father, Jesus, the Son, and Holy Spirit, the Comforter and Teacher are more than I could ever have asked for or deserved.

More so, I have experienced the massive miracles of a changed heart and a transformed mind. I wear skin that has healed from an extensive burn injury and I have learned that scars result from healing. They are no longer open wounds that need care. Jesus chose to carry the reminders of his brutal death on his transformed body. They marked his sacrifice; He was not ashamed of them; He was completely healed, yet they remained—His love for us etched into His skin.

In that, I let go. *God, if more people see Your goodness through the presence of my scars, then I trust You will give me the grace to wear them. If You want to show people Your power to heal through recreating my fingers, then have Your way.*

> JESUS CHOSE TO CARRY THE REMINDERS OF HIS BRUTAL DEATH ON HIS TRANSFORMED BODY.

Maybe there will be a day where a prayer equal to the final blow topples the tree. Perhaps it's about timing or a specific place. I don't know, but I trust what I cannot see, and God's ways are more sophisticated than mine. He is for me, not against me. This, in itself, is a miracle.

Life is also a blessing. I look around and see miracles happening every day.

Every day God gives me what I need—and more. I'm loved; I get to love; I see beauty in my surroundings and in the people whose paths I cross. I see God answering prayers and revealing His character and love to His children.

The list could go on forever when I open my eyes to see from the blades of grass that grow to the warmth of the sun. Sometimes I forget to look; then, I get discouraged, and my hope starts to fade. At some point, I remember all the small miracles—the ones so obvious I missed them. These tiny miracles are more significant than the seemingly impossible ones. In it all, God shows me He is with me, caring for every detail of my life, creating, planning, and dreaming with me, and preparing a way with a future and hope far exceeding my ability to imagine. That's the greatest miracle of all—the god of the universe, caring about me.

"Though the LORD is exalted, he looks kindly on the lowly; though lofty, he sees them from afar. Though I walk in the midst of trouble, you preserve my life." (Psalm 138:6-7 NIV)

PART II

OVERCOMING

6

SCARS

I sat at a dining table outside a hotel in downtown Raleigh, North Carolina, with three people I had just met. One was a woman, about forty years old. She shared pictures of her two sons—her reasons for living. She had severe burns from an act of domestic violence. Her injuries altered her hairline, covered her face and body with scars, and destroyed parts of her fingers. Her mother, who was her caregiver and friend, sat next to me.

On the other side of me sat a man who had very little left of his facial features and his hands. He had been a fireman, and an act of heroism had disfigured him, scarring over 90 percent of his body.

As we chatted, the woman who had been burned looked at the man and me and asked, "How do you handle it when people do more than stare? When they are mean to you and kick you out of stores and restaurants because your looks are disturbing the other customers?"

I was in silent shock as I listened to them relay stories back and forth about when people would not allow them to shop or share a meal out with their families and friends. I was horrified by the way people had talked to them. The store owners, management, and employees had no clue about the circumstances leading up to these disfigurements. They had no idea of the pain these individuals had already endured.

For a while, I felt like I had no right to speak. Because of my surgeries, my hair neatly covered my head. I had a nose, cheekbones, lips, and eyelids; my makeup was just right, and I had carefully picked my outfit to flatter my frame. Then I looked down and saw my right hand without any fingers. I remembered back to the year I wore a pressure mask everywhere I went. I recalled the two years the whole top of my head had no hair and the seven years of surgeries. And I recollected going out in public. The people sitting here with me hadn't seen me that way. They hadn't seen me at my worst. Their stories evoked a feeling of some of their dread.

In the first year following my injury, countless situations happened in public that left me in tears—ignorant comments, stares, mean statements, endless questions, and children running scared from me. But I was never asked to leave. Nobody ever intimated that my absence would be better for the majority.

My surgeries were always away from home. I would stay in a hotel for two weeks following each surgery in case there were any complications. After the first week of healing, I often got cabin fever and was eager to get out of the room. My caregiving friend and I would make outings to local restaurants for a meal, and I would contemplate how my cut-up face must appear to the other customers. But I was never told I was ruining the other patrons' appetites or my presence was unwelcome.

I spoke up to my new friends and shared words my mama told me when she realized how others would view her beautiful first child, who looked different because of a fire. "Charity, you're going to have to teach others how to treat you."

My mother didn't say this to an outgoing, say-anything-anywhere, knows-no-strangers daughter. She said it to the shy daughter, the one who didn't go to new places without a friend and didn't speak until spoken to.

When I took my mama's words to heart, I realized if people were ever going to see who I was, then I was going to have to be brave. I would have to show them—through my dress, body language, and approach to both the mundane and the new, challenging life tests.

I have traveled all over the United States (and to many other countries), conducting business, making new friends, shopping, eating, sightseeing, and discovering some simple truths. I can't always determine how others will treat me. Maybe I never experienced what my new friends were talking about because I never imagined being treated that way.

People do catch me off guard sometimes. They ask me difficult questions, but I quickly realize they are voicing what others wonder but never speak. If I treated them rudely, I'd be treated rudely in return. If I'm waiting for an insult, one will come.

I've noticed when I'm having a bad day, if I'm sick, tired, or emotional, or if I'm focused on myself and think myself unlovely, it's on those days I notice the stares. Something inside me permits others to focus on my differentness.

The rest of the days, I go about my business. I'm focused on my to-do list or the people I'm with, taking time to relate to the cashiers, or smiling at the mother struggling with the toddler in her cart. The thoughts about me being different, people staring at me, or not belonging never cross my mind. If people do stare, I don't notice because I'm not focused on myself. If people treat me differently, they usually treat me nicely because I am nice to them.

Most importantly, I've discovered when I'm okay with me, others are okay with me. That's how it is today, but it wasn't always that way.

LIFE BEYOND THE SCARS

REJECTION

I was sixteen years old, walking down the sidewalk outside my school, on the way to the parking lot, wearing my long, thick hair down. I had an oversized sweater on with colorful leggings and flats. Walking in front of me were two boys from my class; I overheard a slice of their conversation.

"There are no pretty girls here," said the first.

The friend replied, "What about her?" as he nodded in my direction.

"Yeah, but did you see her face?"

He was referring to my acne; it was a problem. I knew it was the reason I didn't have a boyfriend. It was probably why I wasn't popular either.

As a child, I remember having one or two friends. We got along great, or so it seemed. As far as I was concerned, I could never get tired of my friends. Their words didn't offend me. I never thought them boring. I was genuinely interested in their thoughts and feelings. I don't even recall being annoyed by them at all.

I also remember that there was always at least one person who was "the third wheel" in every school I attended. It was a person who generally craved attention. They would jump from group to group. This person acted silly, always had something to say, laughed too loud, spread gossip, and was always there. He or she was annoying; nobody would want them around. Yet, they never seemed to get the hint.

At every school, there was also a person whose hair was never brushed, whose clothes were dirty, and who smelled funny. That person was the punch line to everyone's jokes. He or she was often quiet, withdrawn, and seemed rejected.

One of my biggest fears was that I was one of these people. I believed nobody thought what I had to say was interesting. They were probably just being nice to me and didn't *really* want me around. They might accept me at first, but if they got to know me and found out how boring I was, or how little I knew… Did I smell funny? My clothes were never right, in my opinion, no matter how hard I tried.

I would replay each conversation in my head, searching for what I may have said or done to cause my friends to banish me. I made rules for myself about what I should and shouldn't say or how to act or dress. The rules would hopefully prevent my embarrassment or, most of all, rejection.

No matter how hard I tried to be the person I imagined my peers would like, I always seemed to fall short. Even though I looked fine when I left for school, I did not measure up when I got there and compared myself to the others. My clothes were not name-brand; they weren't the latest style—not even new. I never came up with the right witty statement at the appropriate time. I never seemed to be creative, unique, or confident enough to stand out, be liked, fit in, or *belong*.

I was naturally quiet and reserved, but I also hid behind that. I tried to find the place where I fit in enough but didn't stand out—so I wouldn't be noticed and therefore rejected.

It's funny how, in my life, no matter how much I wanted to blend in, there always seemed to be some uncontrollable circumstance that would draw me out and cause everyone to see me. They would laugh, snicker, or talk about me to each other, and I would try to become invisible again.

This discomfort carried over into my adult life. As I grew older, my list of self-imposed rules grew longer. I persevered, trying to make myself what I imagined everyone else thought I should be. I was concerned I was that squeaky, annoying third wheel—constantly afraid once people found out who I truly was, down deep, I would be alone. I couldn't love myself because *my self* always put me in jeopardy, and it always betrayed me. No matter how hard I was on *myself*, no matter how much I beat *myself* up, *my self* never obeyed; it never made me proud; it always failed. I knew *my self* very well.

When others said they loved me, or when they said I was great, talented, or funny, I wouldn't believe it. I felt they would soon be disappointed with me, but the truth was, I was disappointed with myself. I thought it was kind of them to love me and generous of them to be my friend. I lived in fear that they would say one thing to my face but say something completely different about me in their homes. I would do just about anything to ensure they wouldn't reject me. My newfound scars only reinforced what I already thought of myself. One day, I realized that when I live my life in fear of being rejected, I

- see every person as a potential threat to my self-esteem.

- hear every whisper shared as a secret, spoken about me.

- imagine every snicker or giggle is a joke at my expense.

- believe every conversation has double meanings, laced with pity or ulterior motives.

- translate every opinion into a judgment.

- assume when I walk into the store, everybody's lives pause, and they all turn their attention to my disfigurement.

- presume every scowl is an expressed disapproval of my differences.

- make everything about me.

In all these ways, I am giving over my power to strangers. Consequently, I am giving them control over my life. I created a world centered around my brokenness and reinforcing my loss. It is idolatry that I bow to my perceived opinion of others and skew what I believe about myself, my value, and my worth.

That's not to say there aren't people out there who do stare, do say dumb things, make fun of me, or even misjudge me. How much power do I want to give them? Will I hold the opinion of strangers higher than the views of those who know and love me? Will I live in fear of what others think of me, making that perception more relevant than what God thinks of me?

I get to choose. Rejection steals the best of who I am by reinforcing the worst of what others say about me. Today's challenge is not to allow the worst of what they say to replace the truth of who I am in Jesus Christ. "Normal" got snatched away, and the "new normal" that I've developed and labeled "my life" is still uncharted territory.

It often comforts me to remember that Jesus, God in the flesh, knows what it feels like to be rejected, ridiculed, scarred, and mocked, and yet continues to grace me with His love.

> REJECTION STEALS THE BEST OF WHO I AM BY REINFORCING THE WORST OF WHAT OTHERS SAY ABOUT ME.

"He was despised and rejected by men, a man of sorrows and acquainted with grief; and as one from whom men hide their faces he was despised, and we esteemed him not. Surely he has borne our griefs and carried our sorrows; yet we esteemed him stricken, smitten by God, and afflicted." (Isaiah 53:3-4)

Jesus has borne my grief and carried my sorrows. He has made a way for me to live unafraid of others' opinions and bathed in His unconditional love that never leaves or forsakes me. His love doesn't change—even when I do. He's the one that shows me the way when there is no way. Jesus saved my life, chose me, called me His own, and never rejected me.

COURAGE

I picked my baby sister up from ballet class; she had to be about five or six years old. As I walked in to find her, she was sitting on the floor with a bunch of little girls. They were all giggling as they took off their ballet shoes. I walked up to Laura to see if she needed any help and let her know I was there. The giggling stopped, and the little girls began to whisper.

Completely confused, Laura asked, "Why are they staring at you? What's wrong with them?"

I smiled at the girls and said, "Hello."

To Laura, I continued, "It is normal for kids to stare and wonder about me; they just don't know that I am okay."

"Oh...." Laura said, still not understanding. She hadn't known me to be different, and she had never known me to be "not okay."

"It's okay, Laura. All you have to do is hold my hand and smile at them. If you do that, they will know I'm okay and that I'm safe."

Laura jumped up and grabbed my hand; with a big smile, she informed them, "This is my big sister! She came to pick me up! Bye!" And we walked out hand in hand.

As the years passed, this became a regular thing, even as Laura grew to be a teenager and young adult. Children always wonder and often stare. I place a smile on my face and let them. It can be annoying and awkward at times, but I recognize their minds don't know how to come up with an answer to why I'm different.

So, whenever we walked through Walmart, rode on a train, or traveled all the way across the world, and a little kid would stare, Laura would take my hand and smile at them. With her hand in mine and a smile on her face, we showed them I was okay.

"Have I not commanded you? Be strong and courageous. Do not be afraid; do not be discouraged, for the LORD your God will be with you wherever you go." (Joshua 1:9 NIV)

Before I was injured, I never would have described myself as courageous. We moved from town to town, changing schools frequently. While my parents never allowed our insecurities to excuse us from what we needed to do, those self-doubts were always there taunting me as I stumbled my way through school and life.

I've since learned courage is when

- I go to an event, even though everything in me wants to stay home;

- I share my opinion at the risk of being silenced or mocked;

- I push through and do hard things, even when I want to give up;

- I hold to my values, even when those around me don't;
- I do the "right" thing even when it's not my job;
- I take a risk and step into the unknown;
- I initiate a conversation;
- I take the first step toward a dream;
- I go about my "normal" life wearing my scars.

I drew courage up from down deep, where God resides, giving grace, helping me take the first step. Reminding me even if I stumbled, even if others didn't understand, even if I felt rejected

- He's there.
- He has a plan.
- Nothing is wasted.
- I am absolutely loved.

From this, I began to see and know:

"...With man this is impossible, but with God all things are possible." (Matthew 19:26 NIV)

This framework was where I could find the way through the scars into a life full of possibilities.

I labored to prove to myself and everyone else that I am not "limited," "handicapped," "disabled," or "disfigured." My desire for others to look at me without pity in their eyes motivated me. I didn't want them to look at me and automatically label me as "less than."

* * *

These days, I rarely consider a lot of these things. My thoughts, time, emotions, and words I speak to others revolve around our jobs, homes, to-do lists, health, weather, life events, relationships, food, shopping, etc. I spend very little time acknowledging the scars, the reason they are there, or the difficulty they bring to my life.

However, there are a few times each year I must acknowledge the scars. I bring the story of the accident out of the archives and share it with a curious stranger or a bold child. I take the story with me to a platform reserved for me.

When I find myself overheating, struggling with a lid, bleeding from scratch from an unknown source, explaining my bald spots to a new hairdresser, or noticing other customers at a restaurant who seem to keep looking at my table, I remember the reason. When these situations arise, I pull out my arsenal of coping mechanisms, apply the appropriate one, and quickly move on.

I don't want to get drawn in because I might get stuck there, sucking me into a virtual black hole where there is no hope, life, or laughter—where there is only nothingness filled with unanswered questions.

So, I swallow the lump that rises in my throat. I smile through the embarrassment caused by the spotlight shining on me for something I lived through that shows on the outside. I shelf the frustration and anger that an incident from over twenty-seven years past is now interrupting my ordinary day.

It's become so typical for me to do this; I don't even recognize when I am. I forget that, in the meantime, my shelf is getting filled up. There's inevitably a day when this shelf will be so full; it'll make itself evident. I must acknowledge it and clear the clutter before everything comes tumbling down.

Sometimes, it seems the pile is glaring at me are every time I turn around, and there are seasons when I have to spend more time acknowledging the scars. Then there are times when it seems like years can go by without even remembering the shelf. Yet all of a sudden, it's fuller and messier than I thought.

I'm not saying I haven't overcome, or I haven't healed from my wounds; I have. But healing from an injury still leaves a scar. Scars indicate there was something significant to deal with. Most people have these marks of varying sizes and degrees, but most peoples' battles are hidden; I can't hide mine. Sometimes, I try to deal with them the same way I do wounds. With an emotional injury, I acknowledge it, treat it with prayer, truth, and time. Eventually, it heals, and I move on.

But my scars, and their long-term effect on my life, make themselves so obvious I cannot shelve the feelings that arise in me. Instead, I have to deal with the mess in front of me. I try to pray it away, speak about all the things I'm thankful for, or the ways my life is blessed. I busy myself, creating a distraction from the negative feelings screaming at me. I trace down the lie at the root of the emotions and speak the truth over it. I search for the fear that creates smoke and mirrors and muster up the courage to walk through the discomfort.

The truth is, scars aren't wounds to be healed. They don't need the same treatment. A scar is the evidence of something that was once broken but healed. To pretend the scar itself is the injury is to deny that healing has already happened.

Yes, God can take away the evidence that something ever happened to begin with, whether it's a physical, spiritual, or emotional injury. Jesus kept His scars; they provided evidence to the doubters. Is it possible that if God removed our scars, the validity of our testimony would disappear as well?

To imagine that because I have scars, it means I'm not well or whole is a contradiction to the reality of what a scar represents.

It's interesting how silly humans are. Some disfigurements are cool—the marks acquired in battle, for instance, represent an act of bravery or a near-death experience. Having a defect resulting from an emergency surgery—like heart surgery or an appendectomy—is okay for men; however, women find it a flaw.

The people who most intrigue me are those who cover their bodies with tattoos, using their skin as a canvas to express opinions, creativity, individuality, or to tell their story. Some people look at them with admiration; some feel they have damaged their bodies. However, tattoos have become socially acceptable; I know of pastors and kindergarten teachers who have them.

But, to be *covered* with scars? Even those *covered* with tattoos don't see the irony. People are waiting for the cure, a plastic surgery phenomenon that will take scar tissue and turn it back into baby skin. People don't look at a body covered in scars and view it as evidence of a miracle; they see it as something to be fixed, something to be avoided at all costs.

As a result, we're always trying to get rid of our physical scars. Embracing them doesn't seem to be an option—to me, that would make them part of my identity. I don't want that; I don't want something terrible that I overcame and healed from to be the marker of my whole life.

What if people didn't consider scars as something to be afraid of or pitied, but rather something to be honored?

What if the miracle(s) that allowed the healing, even when it created the scar, was the marker instead?

What if we dealt with scars by declaring miracles?

It truly is a miracle that God created us with the ability to heal. It's also a miracle when:

- bitterness and self-pity are healed through gratitude and praise;

- lack heals through focusing on blessing;

- fear vanishes through perfect love;

- truth demolishes lies;

LIFE BEYOND THE SCARS

- the weak are made strong;
- forgiveness restores relationships.

We can change our perspective, recognizing the presence of a scar is evidence of a miracle.

7

VICTIM VERSUS OVERCOMER

She was about twelve years old. Her mother sat next to Mama and me in the waiting room. We were at the hospital for a follow-up appointment to discuss the next step of my recovery. The girl who sat next to me was from California. She, too, had facial burns, as well as burns all over the rest of her body. She wasn't wearing a mask like I was.

Her mother told my mama, "I know it's hard to see right now, but your daughter seems to be healing well."

"Thank you; she definitely has her challenges. One of the things she's struggling with the most right now is wearing her mouth spreader. It's like a medieval torture device. I cringe when I have to crank it wider. Have you discovered any tips so I can make it more comfortable for her?"

The other mother confided, "I understand how you feel. My daughter cried every time I encouraged her to use her mouth spreader. I just can't make her do it; she's been through so much pain, and she still has more therapy and surgeries to go. The pressure garments and masks create pressure sores; the splints make it hard for her to do anything. I don't want to be the one making her hurt more. I gave up trying to get her to wear her mouth spreader."

"What's the next step for your daughter?" my mama asked.

"She can no longer eat solid food; her mouth won't open far enough anymore because of the scar tissue. She eats through a straw. We are going to discuss surgery options for her."

The mouth spreader's job was to push against the scars as the skin around the mouth healed to help the mouth open wider over time. Without its usage, the scar tissue around the mouth remains rigid and inflexible, restricting movement.

As we continued to talk, something dawned on me. There were garments, devices, splints, and therapy tools highly recommended by the doctors. The hospital provided these tools freely and staff trained parents on how to use them. None of them were comfortable to use; all of them hurt or caused additional challenges to work around, above and beyond the ongoing pain and itching, which came with simply healing from a burn injury.

While I was in the hospital, my parents learned about devices to aid in my recovery and make it smoother in the long run. They decided to listen to the doctors' advice—even if it was uncomfortable for me—to have the best chances for recovery.

The twelve-year-old girl was about a year ahead of me in her recovery time. However, now that this girl's scars were mature enough to start surgeries, she would need more intervention because of the limitations she faced. These problems were still present because it hurt the mom too much to let her daughter experience any more pain—even if it was for her long-term good.

I'm sure you've heard similar stories. I heard them growing up regarding children of divorce or trauma:

- "My child has already been through so much; why wouldn't I buy them every new toy? Maybe it will make up for the fact I can't be around as much."

- "Oh, it's okay if she gets that; look at what she's been through."

- "He can be mad; he doesn't mean it; he's been through so much."

I heard it myself from well-meaning acquaintances. They held me to a different standard than everyone else. As if what I had been through entitled me to bad attitudes, more treats, less responsibility— as if it excused me from lashing out and feeling sorry for myself.

Don't get me wrong; there was a time I needed a lot of care and attention. My life hung in the balance, and I was extremely limited in my ability to function. I needed calories to heal and help from other people to provide nourishment. I required a safe place to grieve and express my frustration regarding the loss I faced and the pain I endured. Learning how to do everyday tasks in new ways was challenging. Surgeries were vital years after my injury, which again required me to have help afterward. These needs all put a lot of attention on my recovery during every part of the process.

Once I started to regain independence and adjust to my new life, I couldn't stay there. It was easy to get in the habit of having all that attention and to let everything revolve around me and my every whim. It was effortless to become the home's temperature, requiring everyone around me to adjust to my needs and wants, regulating their behavior according to me. It was simple to start controlling everyone to maintain my comfort. However, later when I went out into the world, expecting to get everything easily, I quickly realized the world wasn't as concerned about my comfort and convenience as I thought they should be.

In that, I could take on my new condition as my identity. I could wear my labels:

- "Burned girl."

- "The girl with the scars."

- "The girl who lost her fingers."

Labeled this way, anyone who came around me knew they should be careful, sensitive to my plight, and cautious of their words. They should have imagined the daily agony I faced living in this body.

My past then became my present, and I became a victim to my circumstances:

- I couldn't see beyond myself;

- my emotions were stunted;

- my future became dim;

- my relationships weakened;

- the people closest to me let my tragedy engulf their future:

  - causing them to bow to the moment,

  - allowing their life to revolve around me,

  - becoming collateral damage in the same disaster.

A victim's identity is in their injury; every aspect of their life revolves around their lack and worst pain.

"Godly sorrow brings repentance that leads to salvation and leaves no regret, but worldly sorrow brings death." (2 Corinthians 7:10 NIV)

When I had "worldly sorrow" or others had it for me, allowing me to take the easy road instead of the best path for my growth and healing was a disservice. It relegated me to a self-confined prison and required all who wanted to be around me to come to that place to relate to me—allowing me to grow weak and limiting my future to the four walls around me. While it felt safe and predictable, even something I could control, it provided little joy. Life should have surprises, adventures, and, most of all, freedom.

Worldly sorrow searches for someone or something to blame for every bad day I have, for my worst pain, for my lack, even my attitude. It makes me a perpetual victim—not just injured once, but reinjured due to my perspective.

> IT RELEGATED ME TO A SELF-CONFINED PRISON AND REQUIRED ALL WHO WANTED TO BE AROUND ME TO COME TO THAT PLACE TO RELATE TO ME.

When I behaved like a victim, I rarely owned up to my mistakes. Selfishness, name-calling, hatefulness, temper tantrums, and disrespect for authority were easy coping tools. These victim-mindset tools, however, only caused more pain:

- I rarely took responsibility for my self-destructive behavior.

- I hardly ever apologized, constantly shifting the blame away from myself, which caused me never to own my mistakes, blunderings, sins, or failures.

- I felt entitled, always requiring preferential treatment, never accepting "no" as the answer.

- I justified over-spending, over-eating, treats, excess of anything—as something I deserved because of the pain I went through.

- I focused entirely on my comfort and security. I fixated on preventing any further pain to myself, making my pain more urgent than everyone else's.

- I didn't see the pain others endured.

- I didn't grasp the pain I caused.

- I failed to have sympathy.

One of the best things my parents did for me was to stand united and require me to do the hard and painful things for my long-term benefit. It helped me heal faster and encouraged me to take the initiative to regain my independence.

My parents recognized during our childhood that discipline, while challenging, was necessary for our growth and well-being. They taught us to obey, even when we didn't like it, and work hard, even when we didn't want to. And, they instilled in us the word "no." No meant no. It was not a negotiation—we couldn't have everything we wanted when we wanted it.

These were valuable lessons that greatly aided in my recovery.

"...because the Lord disciplines the one he loves, and he chastens everyone he accepts as his son." (Hebrews 12:6 NIV)

* * *

Several months after I returned home from the hospital, I was ready to buy my first car. At eighteen, I wanted to step back into my life. In our family, our parents required us to have the money saved before purchasing a car. We would pay in cash, with enough savings left over to cover the insurance and maintenance. I had money and savings left over, so my dad and I started to shop around.

We found a little Subaru Justy, a subcompact hatchback, that was just the right price. But it had a manual transmission. It would be hard to drive as I no longer had fingers on my right hand. My dad hesitated as he checked the car over, making sure it was mechanically sound. Meanwhile, I insisted I could learn to drive a stick shift. We sealed the deal. The car was mine.

My dad took me out to some dirt roads and proceeded to teach me. We struggled our way through the lessons as the car stalled over and over again. I fought to turn the wheel with my still weak left hand. My dad thought it through; a knob on the steering wheel would help me steer. Adding a lever to my key could assist me in starting the car with my right hand. With how often I had to restart the vehicle, I needed these minor tweaks. As far as stalling and grinding gears, that was just going to take practice.

A couple of hours and many frustrated tears later, I had it down. I was proud of my accomplishment; I had learned how to drive a manual transmission, and that would give me more freedom and flexibility over time.

While I was on cloud nine, feeling one step closer to "normal," unbeknownst to me, my dad was chided by the other adults in my family for forcing me to learn to drive a standard. He never defended himself—telling them I insisted, and he never said a word to me at the time. He kept this scolding to himself because he didn't feel sorry for me. Instead, he helped me do hard things. I am now able to drive any car I hop into.

Later down the road, he taught me how to hook up my horse trailer and back it up—giving me another level of abilities. He instilled in me a sense of independence and freedom, which in turn opened the door to adventures, whereas being stuck in "worldly-sorrow" would have withheld me.

* * *

I love stories about those who overcome; I think most of us do. The reality is, everyone I respect and most things I read or watch are about others who have accomplished incredible feats, despite their circumstances. It's not just cheering for the underdog; it's valuing what is right, true, and just, despite the obstacles.

As I listen to the tales of the extraordinary acts by regular people facing unpredictable situations, I find myself thinking, *what would I do if I were in their place?* I hope if I were faced with the choice to stand up for great injustice perpetrated on the innocent or a life and death decision on someone else's behalf or an insurmountable challenge that I would be able to stand against the injustice and even turn it around. I would stare death in the face and defeat it. I would find the strength somewhere within me to pull the sword from the stone.

Every day there we hear about heroes who . . .

- fight for, protect, and defend our freedom—regardless of the cost;

- commit to our safety and protection;

- rescue us;

- heal us;

- defend us;

- shield children from bullets;

- are brave enough to challenge the rich and powerful.

I love to be inspired by ordinary people who have overcome: cancer, amputation, paralysis, mental and physical disabilities, stereotypes, terminal illness, etc.

I see these stories on social media or on the news; they are discussed over coffee with friends. My days can seem grueling, an unrelenting routine of everyday existence. Then I hear of horrific events that bring forward such grief for my fellow man. And I count my blessings, hold my loved ones closer, and step back into my regular, mundane life.

None of us wants tragedy to knock on our door. Many pray for protection and enforce all the measures of precaution available to them. We don't want to see our loved ones struggle or be in pain. We want good things—a life filled with healthy, fulfilling relationships; laughter; joy; contentedness; and satisfaction.

I believe we all want to feel a sense of victory as well. We want to know there is a hero somewhere inside us, an inner strength to fight despite the odds. Even if our greatest enemy is the voice inside us chipping away at our security, confidence, hope, and faith, resulting in a life where we are just trying to keep our head above water, we want to overcome.

I don't believe conquering is reserved for those who have a tragedy flung upon them. I think it is something we all can experience.

Overcoming consists of...

- having the courage to face our fears, stresses, anxieties, wounds, enemies, addictions, and relationships;

- dealing with our moods, thoughts, and behaviors, despite our negative feelings;

- the willingness to bring the truth to every part of our life;

- and the tenacity to let light, truth, righteousness, and justice do their work.

These qualities and behaviors help us succeed. God loves overcomers; He gives us everything we need to become one with Him. He knows it is a battle with a series of victories and losses. He knows there are costs to surmounting trials, but He also knows the joy of victory. He greatly desires for us to walk in triumph and freedom.

The measure of faith God gave me, mixed with the ingredients He instilled in my life when He formed me in my mother's womb and the truths established, helped pave the way to live as an overcomer.

Having tools for the quest does not negate pain, bad days, tears, confusion, darkness, and torment. Warriors still have to go into battle against the enemy of their soul—whose purpose is to separate them from the love of God—using any means necessary. Overcomers win; they come out stronger and wiser after their fights are over. They then take the tools gained in the skirmishes and help others fight—for God's glory and for personal freedom.

The car accident, the burn injuries, healing, learning to love myself, and receiving God's love were the first of many battles. They set a foundation. As more trials came, I had something to stand on. God had been victorious on my behalf in the past; He would be there for me in this present situation.

* * *

At the age of 22, I decided it was time to go to college, step out on my own, and put the accident and the significant interruption it caused in the past. Because I had been out of school for four years, I decided to go to community college to get back in the school groove with less pressure and no competition.

I chose a community college in Tucson because I planned to transfer from there to the University of Arizona. Additionally, I would be only one hundred miles from my grandparents, making the move even sweeter.

I was excited to resume a "normal" life. I set up a home, got my classes lined up, and stepped out on my own to maneuver into my new life. I remember the first day of classes. It was the first time I had stepped into a group of strangers all alone, committed to sitting with them for hours over the course of the semester. I imagined all the friends I would make, coffee dates, study groups, weekend parties at my house—"normal" college life.

By now, four years after the accident, I had been to a lot of new places. I had traveled on my own and with my family; I had been to malls and amusement parks; I had tried new things, met people, and made friends. Most of these adventures were with others—at least one family member or friend as a companion.

Now reality came crashing down on me. I sat in the school campus courtyard, waiting for my next class, holding back the tears that I knew, if let loose, would come in waves, realizing I just signed myself up to spend years in an uncontrolled environment. This situation wasn't at all like the other first days of school I had experienced growing up, moving from one place to another.

Those first days at college were eye-opening. I had been learning to live with my new body and adjusting to my ever-evolving looks. However, these people didn't know me or my story; they weren't prepared for my presence. I felt like I needed to warn them. I wanted to wear a T-shirt with my "before" picture on it, so people could see who I once was—that I was really a beautiful person.

People weren't mean to me. In fact, some tried to cross the barrier of my differences and reach out. When I was the "new kid" last time, I was surrounded by teenagers asking questions, guys flirting with me, and friends sharing common ground.

I guess I expected college to be the same, but the reality that it wasn't struck me hard that day. I realized all the moving around as a kid, being noticed, and being different—when all I wanted to do was fit in and not stand out—was a preparation for my future.

Now, there's not a place I can go where people won't notice me, and my looks won't bring me attention; I can't blend in. So I've had to learn to accept the spotlight.

SUPER SURVIVOR

I didn't want to portray being a "victim" to my injury. I was actively working to overcome it; however, this was a process for me. It was a long course filled with many things to learn about myself, my responses, and my mindsets.

I don't think anyone in my life could say with definition, "This is how we overcome." Resources in the form of a string of friends who were overcomers were available to observe and guide me, even though we were all going about it in different ways, for various reasons.

Seven years after my injury, I was still living in Tucson. I had borderline chronic fatigue at twenty-five years old. Desiring a master's degree in art and psychology, I took my general education classes before specifying my major. In addition to my education, I also

- started a non-profit organization;
- maintained a large home;
- cared for my dog and my horse;
- rode three to five days a week;
- planned for surgeries during every school break, despite having already endured over twenty operations;
- visited my grandparents on the weekends;
- talked to my parents and siblings every day;
- tried to be the perfect friend, daughter, granddaughter, and sister;
- felt a need to prove to everyone their investment in my life was a sound one;
- became a "Super Survivor;"
- believed I was failing if I didn't meet what I thought were everyone's expectations for my life, especially those who loved me the most;
- felt alone and tormented;
- plagued myself with guilt that I hadn't done enough, said the right thing, or acted appropriately;
- had many rules I lived by;

- wanted to make sure I repaid those who helped me, especially if I was going to ask for help again;

- desired never to be a burden again;

- sought not to cause my family any more pain than I already had.

I wanted to make sure it never cost those who were kind enough to be my friends; I didn't want them to regret being close to me. The fire had stripped me of any "normal" existence. It took away my plans for the future, my beauty, my strength, and it took away the little confidence I had. Miraculously, I had survived. My family and friends greatly sacrificed their time and effort to help me regain my independence, know I was loved, and look forward to a future.

I struggled with many questions:

- "Why did I live?"

- "What was my purpose?"

- "What if…?"

- "Would a man ever be able to love and accept me as I am?"

I concluded that if I could help others, it was okay that I was burned, scarred, and disfigured. A noble conclusion, but what if I wasn't able to help others?

* * *

It was a February day, and my house had just sold. I was driving back from Southern California, where I had attended a wedding. I cried the whole way home. I was wrung out, alone, and didn't have any hope of escaping my torment. An ounce more responsibility felt like it would crush me, and I didn't know if I would be able to recover. I couldn't handle anything more.

Calling my mother to ask for her help from 800 miles away or even admit I needed it was extremely difficult for me. Previously needing so much support, I never wanted to ask again. I was sure I had exceeded my quota for a lifetime.

My mother brought my little brother and sister out, helped me pack up my house, and move it to storage; then we drove to Colorado. "Super Survivor" had just fallen from her pedestal. I was completely overwhelmed—heartbroken by thoughts swarming through my head. I felt like a disappointment to all those I loved the most.

As I later shared my heartbreak with a friend, she told me, "You've never taken the time to heal emotionally from your accident or to grieve your loss." I wasn't sure about that; I had cried many tears since the accident.

I did know that I was tired of being an adult and making decisions that affected the rest of my life. I was tired of trying to be strong. I wanted to be a kid again, letting my parents make the decisions. I didn't want to be responsible anymore.

I stayed in my parents' home for months. I did little things—straightening the house in the mornings, babysitting the kiddos after school, running errands for Mama. In a way, I couldn't believe that I was reduced to this after six years of living on my own. It resembled losing my independence at seventeen. I felt like a teenager again, with the same longing for a future and the same struggle to know who I was. Here I grieved the years of "normal" growth, exchanged for surgeries.

Slowly it dawned on me that my friend was right. I thought if I gathered all the pieces of what I thought a "normal" life looked like: taking steps forward, having surgeries, going out in public, traveling, having my own home, getting an education—and put them together, then I would be all better.

I worked so hard at trying to attain a successful image. If one piece was missing from my picture, I thought I was a failure. At twenty-five, I began to disassemble the puzzle of what I thought I was and all I wanted to be, to discover who I really was underneath.

Over the next few months, I started to analyze the pieces. My parents had allowed me into their home. They covered my needs and didn't even seem to be put out by my intrusion. My grandparents still loved me. While I knew I was disappointing everyone by not going to school, it wasn't the end of the world. I began to recognize that even when I was weak and needy, had nothing to give, and didn't have all the answers, they still loved me.

When I tried to please everyone, I was a constant disappointment to myself. No human can follow every rule to keep everyone happy all the time. When my focus was on everyone else's hopes for my future, then I lost sight of the One who held my destiny in His hands.

The biggest thing for me to learn was who I was underneath—regardless of degrees, titles, hobbies, goals, dreams, wisdom, clothing, weight, or the correct answers. The person who was simply me was enough and had incredible value even though I was marred.

> WHEN I TRIED TO PLEASE EVERYONE, I WAS A CONSTANT DISAPPOINTMENT TO MYSELF.

8
FACING FEARS

When I was in eighth grade, I had a part in the play "Bye, Bye, Birdie." As a fainting fan, all I had to do was scream and faint when Birdie walked into the room. I was excited to be in the play, to be "cool,"—maybe this was my ticket—but I was terribly shy. I was afraid I wouldn't be able to faint "right," and the audience would laugh and make fun of me. So I dropped out of the play.

When I was in college, I had to give a required oral presentation for my Biology class. Prepared as I was—having written my report, made my visual aids, and studied my material—when it was my turn to speak, I stood up in front of the class, and my mind went blank. I had spent months with this small group of people; I should have been able to do this. But the words wouldn't come. Eventually, I stumbled my way through, and somehow, I passed.

Next, a youth and family ministry invited me to help staff a mission trip to London. The group took youth overseas every summer to serve through performing arts. The community taught us choreographed dances and dramas, we then went and performed in various locations. Dancing was the easy part. We were also encouraged to share our testimonies publicly. This assignment consisted of standing in front of strangers and telling them what God had done in our lives in one to three minutes. It was the terrifying part.

I knew God had guided me to go on this trip; I had to participate. I knew everyone was already looking at me—they always did. Cognizant that I had a striking testimony about God saving my life and giving me the grace to live it, there were no excuses. Regardless of my fears—the fact that my voice would shake—I needed to speak anyway. I was part of a team, and everybody on the team participated.

I still stumbled my way through but didn't give up. Every time I offered my testimony, people thanked me for sharing. Somehow, my story helped people; it gave them hope.

Since then, I've spoken countless times—at churches, meetings, on television, at events, baccalaureates, and many more mission trips. I can't say I'm a great public speaker now, nor can I say I'm comfortable with a microphone in my hand. What I do know is when I face my fear and share God's goodness in my life—He meets me in that place. There I heal a little more and become stronger, while those listening are hopefully encouraged and get to know a bit more of God's goodness.

"Do not fear, for I have redeemed you; I have summoned you by name; you are mine." (Isaiah 43:1 NIV)

I feel like I need to clarify a little bit. I had given my life to God at seventeen years old. While I experienced miracles and His faithfulness during my recovery, I can't say I absolutely knew how to connect with God yet.

My mother did. She taught that praying, going to church, and reading the Bible was part of being a good Christian. In my young adult life, I tried to do those things—I owed it to God.

I left Tucson feeling like a failure. I couldn't see past myself. I felt completely out of control. I questioned everything in my life from my weight to my relationships, my career choices, and my future. Even in that, I thought I was strong, full of faith. Others repeatedly told me how much God loves me, that I was beautiful (inside and out), and that I was a miracle. Later, I heard that someone would love me, and he would be an amazing man.

I know the people who told me these things had good intentions. I knew their words were heartfelt, but they didn't bring me longed-for peace, joy, or comfort. Nothing in my life resembled that. I felt I wasn't the Christian I was supposed to be. Tormented by my thoughts, emotions overwhelmed me, and I was full of compromise. Criticism ran through my head all the time, declaring to me the reasons why I may be rejected:

- "You'll never be good enough."

- "Once they know who you really are, they'll stop being your friend."

- "It's those extra ten pounds. That's why nobody's attracted to you."

- "They have to love you because they're Christians or family."

- "You're just damaged goods."

I prayed, repented, read devotionals, and memorized Scripture, but, honestly, it wasn't working. I felt like my mustard seed of faith was a dud. I had no clue how I was going to be what everyone thought I should be.

Regardless of what anyone saw—that I was brave, intelligent, creative, hopeful, and an inspiration, on the inside, I was a normal girl with the same feelings, thoughts, insecurities, and concerns that others have. My injury, my scars—they weren't the issue at all. They just pointed out the fact there was an issue. I was lost; I had no clue who I was. I didn't know how to figure that out.

Yes, I could tell God everything I was thinking and feeling. He knew it all anyway, but that wasn't the whole answer. A relationship cannot be a one-sided conversation, and I couldn't hear His side. I read the promises but felt they didn't apply to me for one reason after another.

I believed His word was true. I saw what He did in the lives of others. His goodness, miracles, restoration, and redemption were undeniable. My conclusion was those people had some favor, some key I couldn't find. While I knew He was the answer—that He was the only way I would find peace, joy, and wholeness in my life—I had no idea how to get there.

I would go to church seeking comfort, looking for real peace, only to leave in tears. I went to the "right" place and did the "right" things, prayed the "right" prayers, only to find myself still feeling alone. If anyone saw the pain tearing my heart apart piece by piece, they didn't take the time to bind up my gaping wound; they didn't know how. Their words and hugs were momentary, and I would return home feeling forgotten, knowing nobody understood what was going on inside of me.

Churches were full of beautiful people who appeared to have blessed lives—people with the right looks, the right clothes, happy marriages, happy children, joy, love—everything I wanted. I concluded they had those things because they had made the right choices in their life.

Those people must not have broken any of the commandments; they weren't like me. I was damaged goods. I kept hoping I could have the freedom they had, but my attempts at Bible reading and tearful prayers weren't resulting in the life I hoped for. I knew God forgave all sin; He "so loved the world," and that included me. The part where there was "life abundant," where there was joy, peace, and freedom must have been reserved for other people—not me.

I had waited and hoped for each surgery to unveil the person I once was. Seven years and twenty-some-odd surgeries hadn't done that yet.

I continually prayed but found little relief. I needed more. I listened to pastors and knew they were getting insight from spending time with God, having a real connection. I saw people, ordinary people—not ministers—who seemed to have abundant joy. They didn't seem to be slogging their way through Scripture like I was. They had beautiful lives.

I started to fear I would do the "good Christian" thing the rest of my life and never experience what others seemed to feel.

* * *

When I returned to Colorado, staying with my parents, I started to get involved with a young adult Bible study group. I witnessed people my age who had horrific pasts, but there was something different about them than other Christians I had seen.

They were overcomers—free—people who knew who they were. And they were openly sharing their struggles and what God was teaching them. For some reason, they let me be a part of their group.

These new friends spoke without shame. I remember hearing them describe fears they had, thoughts they would struggle with, emotions that crept up on them. I hadn't heard Christians talk about these things before. They were describing the very things I felt.

Once God forgave me, I thought I wasn't supposed to feel or think negative, ungrateful, or angry things anymore. I was beating myself up every day, trying to make myself behave as I thought I should. No matter how hard I tried, I wasn't seeming to get anywhere because I wasn't looking at the deep-seated reasons for my discontent. I wasn't looking for the root as it grew stronger, went deeper, and took more and more work to maintain. The guilt, shame, and condemnation I felt were constant and heavy.

As I spent more and more time with my new friends, heard their stories and their struggles, listened to them pray for each other, watched as they applied Scripture to real life instead of simply spewing memory verses—I began to open up to them. They started gently showing me areas of my life where I misunderstood God's character.

Normal but broken thought patterns in my life were pointed out to me, backed up by the Word of God. I had a foundation of faith, but there were cracks in my base. I had built my life on that imperfect foundation.

God used these friends to open my eyes to who He is and what His love can accomplish in our lives. He did it in a way I could understand—a way I could learn how to live this faith without being religious or self-righteous.

These young people saw how broken I was. In leaving my present circumstances for even a little while, it was as if a light came on, and I could see. At first, the light was small and dim, quickly covered by darkness, but it was real. Just because something was dimming the light didn't mean the light had gone away. These people were brave enough to tell me the truth.

Honestly, up until that point in time in my life, very few people dared to correct my perspective of life. Many felt I had already been through too much, so they just tiptoed around me.

"Then we will no longer be infants, tossed back and forth by the waves, and blown here and there by every wind of teaching and by the cunning and craftiness of people in their deceitful scheming. Instead, speaking the truth in love, we will grow to become in every respect the mature body of Him who is the head, that is, Christ. From Him, the whole body, joined and held together by every supporting ligament, grows and builds itself up in love, as each part does its work." (Ephesians 4:14-16 NIV)

* * *

Fear is the opposite of faith. I remember hearing that somewhere. In fact, fear is the enemy's weapon to undermine belief, and one of the main tactics used to separate us from God. When we walk in doubt, we are putting our trust in something other than God; we cannot have faith and fear at the same time. While I heard all of that, I didn't know what it meant. Regardless, it stuck with me.

As I learned to apply God's word to my life, I was shocked to discover I was full of angst. I had built so much of my life around my anxiety. The funny thing is, I thought I was brave and courageous. I mean, look what I had lived through!

Early on in the hospital, I decided it would be unreasonable to be terrified of ever getting in a car again. Even though a seatbelt had messed up my day, I still needed to wear one. They do save more lives than they hurt.

I also didn't want to freak out when I heard words like "fire" or "burn."

I didn't want people to walk on eggshells around me or live the life of a recluse.

Hospital and doctor visits would be necessary for years to come, so I couldn't allow myself to fear these visits, needles, surgeries, blood, or wound care. It would be self-defeating.

So, I quickly extinguished those fears. It wasn't easy to climb into a car the first time after my accident or allow my seatbelt to go over me, but I did it. Allowing myself to travel the road our accident happened on took months, but I wouldn't let distress keep me away. I bravely endured all my treatments and submitted to my therapy.

Those horrors, however, were just the first layer. They were the most obvious, yet they were an indicator of what type of survivor I would be. Now I realized there were more layers of fear upon which I based my life decisions— educational, financial, relational, and even spiritual choices.

I was beginning to recognize I wasn't just afraid of what people thought of me; I was jam-packed full of trepidation.

Every move or decision I made, every word out of my mouth, dripped with dread. This timidity was part of the reason my conversations with God remained one-sided. I was worried that if I stopped to listen, I would hear how weary He was of me, and God Himself, the Savior of the world, would reject me.

These fears had already led me into a life with numerous co-dependent, painful relationships and a life riddled with guilt, lies, and confusion. Uneasiness was dictating every step of my life; it was taking away peace and joy, exhausting me, driving me, and causing chaos. It was distorting the picture of who I was and who God was. I had no idea fear was there, and it had been there my whole life. Now I had two choices. I could begin to see it for what it was—and dismantle it piece by piece—or I could pretend it wasn't a big deal—it wasn't my reality—and allow it to continue in my life until it pulled me apart.

I was afraid of

- rejection,
- loneliness,
- being:
    - misunderstood,
    - accused of things that never entered my mind,
    - invisible,
    - useless,
- failing,
- making mistakes,
- rendering the wrong decisions,
- the opinions of others,
- not being loved.

Living my life to please others—an impossible feat—had led to me being overwhelmed, stressed, and anxious about everything. If left in my heart, these fears would eventually paralyze me and cause me so much pain; I would find nobody trustworthy to relate to, even God.

All of this is the purpose of doubt, the intent of the enemy. Every time a familiar fear tries to rise and confine me, I hear a voice saying,

- "Do not be afraid, for I am with you;" (Isaiah 43:5 NIV)

- "Charity, 'Be strong and courageous...'" (Joshua 1:6 NIV)

- "For God has not given us a spirit of fear, but of power and of love and of a sound mind." (2 Timothy 1:7 NKJV)

Then, I repent. Because allowing angst to make my choices is sin. It is not keeping God first. So, I step into the authority given to me through Christ. I recognize that fear is a demon to resist and to cast out of my life. In 2 Timothy, it's referred to as a "spirit of fear."

"Submit yourselves, then, to God. Resist the devil, and he will flee from you." (James 4:7 NIV)

"As you go, proclaim this message: 'The kingdom of heaven has come near.' Heal the sick, raise the dead, cleanse those who have leprosy, drive out demons. Freely you have received; freely give." (Matthew 10:7-8 NIV)

Mustering up my strength and stepping beyond my discomfort while trusting God is more significant than all my concerns, enabling me to grab hold of His immeasurable love for me and others. The result is less room for fear—instead, trust in God will drive it out.

"There is no fear in love [dread does not exist], but full-grown (complete, perfect) love turns fear out of doors and expels every trace of terror! For fear brings with it thought of punishment, and [so] he who is afraid has not reached the full maturity of love [is not yet grown into love's complete perfection]." (1 John 4:18 AMP)

Fear reduces love to a mere word instead of a key element—the massive power behind life. As I became a student of God's love and began to understand it better, there was less room for despair.

COMFORT ZONES

"Do you girls want to go for a walk with me?" Granny asked.

"Yes!" we excitedly responded.

"Okay, put your shoes on and grab a bottle of water."

While we ran off to get ready, she proceeded to pack a few sandwiches and some homemade cookies. These outings were a regular occurrence when we visited Granny. She lived at the base of Miller Canyon in Southern Arizona. She loved to hike and be outdoors; she knew all of the trails like the back of her hand. To her, a daily walk was two miles up and then back down—something we regularly forgot in the excitement of going on an excursion.

"Granny, I'm tired. Can we take a break?" I asked.

"Granny, my legs hurt," Roseanna piped in. Meanwhile, Christy was skipping along.

"Okay, girls, let's stop and have a drink of water."

Christy found the first big rock to sit down. We each had a Rubbermaid water bottle frozen with some water in it, then with more water added to it to start melting the ice. It tasted so good.

After a few minutes, we were back on our feet again, trudging up the mountain. Our little legs tired more quickly the higher up we got. The complaints would become more frequent. The breaks became shorter. Then, we would arrive.

"Okay, girls, let's find a place to sit down," Granny would say.

The creek ran by; the trees provided shade, and we could smell the pine needles that blanketed the ground at our feet. Squirrels chattered as they hopped from tree to tree. Birds called to each other. Granny knew every type of bird.

"Isn't this beautiful, girls?" Granny asked as she handed out our sandwiches. We all nodded. It was fantastic. This adventure was why we said yes to the walk. While we were hiking up, we kept wishing Granny would get tired and turn around, but she never got tired, maybe because she knew what was waiting on the other side of the long walk.

Sometimes, we took off our socks and shoes and played in the creek for a little while, enjoying the spot Granny called her favorite place.

"Okay, girls, time to head back!" Begrudgingly, we put our socks and shoes back on and followed her along the trail. We never needed as many breaks going down the mountain. The return trip never seemed as long as the hike up. All of us fondly remember the places we got to see when we went for a walk with Granny.

* * *

A large part of facing my fears and embracing my life was stepping outside my comfort zone. Every comfort zone differs significantly from person to person. Generally, I'm not easily bothered by things like the weather, a hard seat, or waiting in lines. I can push past my discomfort for the sake of someone else's need—like caring for sick loved ones or holding a crying baby. When I feel it may help someone, I'll work long hours doing tedious jobs. Suppose there's a problem I'm facing. In that case, I'll keep going back to it over and over from different directions until I find the solution. To me, it's a lot like pain tolerance.

Because I experienced a tremendous amount of distress for an extended time, I have a higher tolerance than most. In my life, this means I may be hurting and not register the irritation until it gets pretty bad. That can be a bad thing—to not notice physical or emotional pain until it is a significant wound—as it will require more time and attention to heal correctly. It would require less effort if noticed and cared for at the early onset.

My healthcare providers pushed me far outside my comfort zone when I was injured and admitted to the hospital. My world went from relatively quiet and predictable to entirely and literally out of my control. Others made decisions regarding every aspect of my care for me. The door to my room was a revolving one where stranger after stranger came in and peered under my sheet at my bandaged body. I had no secrets. Caregivers charted every action. I needed assistance for even the slightest movement. Discomfort was a constant companion, continually remaining in my line of sight.

The person that I want to be is...

- Fearless

- Free

- Compassionate

- Helpful

- Spontaneous

- Fun-Loving

- Generous

- Wise

- Faithful

- Reliable

- Loving

- Hopeful

- Full of life

- Whole

To be that kind of person, I have to be willing to face both my fears and the unknown:

- Letting go of the deep desire to control the outcome and plan the future.

- Stepping outside of my small, safe, and predictable world.

- Allowing myself to receive the unexpected.

Facing the unknown requires taking my trust in God to another level and fully believing He has good plans for me. It's obeying Him and His word, even when it's hard—expecting that the outcome will produce something far better than I could make on my own. Living with the hope that although life may be challenging right now, on the other side of the struggle, I find more freedom, and I may be able to show liberty to others.

For me, saying "yes" to life and opportunities as they come my way is not letting fear make my decisions. I've discovered I'm stronger than I ever realized. And my life has been fuller than I ever imagined it could be. In leaving my comfort zone,

- I've learned many new skills.

- I've met incredible people and been inspired by their lives.

- I've been able to travel to many places in the world.

- I've experienced dreams coming true.

- I've received gifts and favors far beyond what I deserve.

- I have healthy, fulfilling relationships.

- I get to help others.

- I have freedom and purpose.

- I know what matters.

- I see God's love, even in the storms.

- I can bravely search for an unknown destiny, filled with faith, expecting miracles.

VULNERABILITY

"My brothers and sisters, if one of you should wander from the truth and someone should bring that person back, remember this: Whoever turns a sinner from the error of their way will save them from death and cover over a multitude of sins." (James 5:19-20 NIV)

There is a crucial ingredient to experiencing true freedom. Whether it's demolishing fears, exposing lies, resisting temptations, or having a pure heart and a clean mind, I had to learn what repentance meant; and a big part of that meant being vulnerable.

In my torment, I confessed to God all I had done wrong—all I was aware of anyway. I would repent; I would try to change—only to disappoint myself repeatedly. My misdeeds constantly danced through my mind, leaving a muddy trail with filthy words and constant frustration at my continual weakness.

As long as my confessions remained between myself and God alone, I was limited to

- my broken interpretation of God's word and the power it held;

- the amount of Scripture I had learned and assimilated into my relatively short life;

- my life experiences;
- my education;
- my understanding;
- my perception of the world around me;
- the amount of light which had broken through the darkness;
- living off of crumbs instead of daily bread.

There was a point in time when I could no longer hide my inner turmoil; it was leaking out onto those I loved the most, and others were starting to notice. That's when I tasted a new level of vulnerability. My sister Christy was with me on my first mission trip to London. I snapped at her in my embarrassment as I struggled through learning the choreographed dances that accompanied our outreaches.

My insecurities screamed at me. It took every ounce of courage I had to stay there with people my age—physically beautiful people—a constant reminder of my limitations. They ministered, served others, and seemed to hear God's word.

The leaders saw my actions toward my sister. My facade started to unravel. They gently began asking questions about my life to understand the breakdown in the relationship I had with my sister. They asked pointed questions. I couldn't divert them or lie; they saw. It started coming out I was in an unhealthy friendship that was bordering on abusive. In my attempts to help others, I was getting hurt.

While it was extremely uncomfortable to share the most shameful moments of my life, they did not judge me. They recognized what I was struggling through, the ways people had mistreated me. They sympathized that I didn't know how to cope; I had no tools. I'm sure my fear of rejection flashed at them like

MY FACADE STARTED TO UNRAVEL.

a neon light across my forehead. Yet, they understood that discomfort would complicate matters, causing me to say yes to things I didn't want to do and dreading ever rejecting or hurting anybody.

As I shared what only God had heard previously, they began to explain that I wasn't merely a victim to my circumstances. I had a part to play in my pain, and for that, I needed to take responsibility and repent.

> *"Therefore confess your sins to each other and pray for each other so that you may be healed. The prayer of a righteous person is powerful and effective." (James 5:16 NIV)*

This communication was when I began to understand the power of vulnerability. This nurturing was when my life started to change. Regardless of how much I was trying to do all the "right" things, according to my understanding, I could still get it all wrong. When I saw that no matter how hard I tried, what I had lived through, or how much I had braved, I realized:

> *"We are all infected and impure with sin. When we display our righteous deeds, they are nothing but filthy rags. Like autumn leaves, we wither and fall, and our sins sweep us away like the wind." (Isaiah 64:5 NLT)*

And God met me in that place. I began to see how I had built my life with a misunderstanding of what loving others meant. I expected God, friends, and family to see all my weaknesses, failures, and mistakes—and then discard me. But that didn't happen.

> *"If we confess our sins, he is faithful and just and will forgive us our sins and purify us from all unrighteousness." (1 John 1:9 NIV)*

My sin was real; it hurt me and others, and it set me up for a life of misery. Once I opened my heart to admit the fact that, regardless of my heart, intentions, or outward actions, I had accepted sin, along with the fears and lies which held it in place, there was a domino effect where I analyzed every thought, behavior, and response.

Regardless of my appearance, demeanor, or the actual number of "bad" things I did, many of my actions were motivated by sin. In tackling the fundamental issues, I discovered I was forgiven—more than others would imagine I could be. So much more than I deserved.

In that process, my love grew. It was as if—for every fear confronted and lie replaced—space was made available for love.

"I tell you, her sins—and they are many—have been forgiven, so she has shown me much love. But a person who is forgiven little shows only little love." (Luke 7:47 NIV)

I discovered how easily I had come to accept sin, how quickly it could take me places I never wanted to go, and how deeply it could injure those I loved the most. As God revealed this to me, my compassion and understanding for others and their entanglements grew. No longer could I judge them or me. The slippery slope, like quicksand, lies in the path of every person's journey and presents itself, disguised, at any given time.

Here is where I feel I began to start healing. In James 5, it states that when we confess our sins to one another and pray for each other, we'll be healed. That's true in my life. I needed to

- share my struggles with others.

- learn who I am and who God is.

- know that other people, too, had gone through painful, hard things and had overcome them.

- remember that I am just as valuable, loved, and precious to God as those I think have it all together.

In facing my fear, being vulnerable, and sharing what was going on with me and what I was learning, something amazing would happen. It would help others, as well.

Condemnation is not from God, although it was my constant companion. It was counterfeit to conviction. Conviction brings with it the discipline that helps me grow, while condemnation beats me down in shame and guilt.

"For God did not send his Son into the world to condemn the world, but to save the world through him." (John 3:17 NIV)

That's what makes God and those who serve Him safe.

God's fruit is not disease, disability, chaos, confusion, offense, resentment, anger, bitterness, pity, or hatred. If I blame God for any of these things, wondering why He put them on me, I am pointing the finger at the wrong party. For He is the one who

- redeems, transforms, restores, creates, heals, perfects, and loves.

- takes me out of the mess and pain I find myself in—whether it is a mess I made, a mess I was born into, or a mess someone else made and dragged me into.

- makes beauty out of ashes.

In identifying with Christ and His suffering on my behalf, I have a very close-up, personal perspective of what He endured. This knowledge causes me to love Him even more; it increases my gratitude. In tasting death, overlaying that the wages of sin are death, and knowing what it feels like and where it leads—why would I purposely sin, putting myself on a path I intimately know will lead to physical suffering? Once clean, I don't want to blatantly and intentionally dirty myself.

"Don't you see how wonderfully kind, tolerant, and patient God is with you? Does this mean nothing to you? Can't you see that his kindness is intended to turn you from your sin?" (Romans 2:4 NLT)

For me, that's how to cross over from overcoming to thriving and living a life of freedom. Abandoning my comfort zone, embracing my fear, being vulnerable, and repenting allowed me to see a glimpse of who God is. In beginning to know Him, I learn more and more who I am.

I may fear losing my reputation or people's trust in me when they learn about my failures and weaknesses. The people I respect the most are those who acknowledge their mistakes, apologize when they are wrong, and ask forgiveness when they've hurt another.

"God opposes the proud but shows favor to the humble." (James 4:6 NIV)

"Humble yourselves before the Lord, and he will lift you up." (James 4:10 NIV)

9

LIES AND TRUTHS

"This isn't going to work; I think we need to step back and just be friends." I said as gently as I could.

"What do you mean? I thought we were going to get married. That's why I moved here. That's why I stopped my life. I'm not sure that I can 'just be friends,'" Leo responded.

I was twenty-six years old. I met my boyfriend preceding the funeral of a dear family friend, Uncle Elmer; he was the nephew. I had been helping the Aunt Betsy and her daughter Sonya with the preparations. He and I had been paired up to take care of the details.

Since the accident, guys hadn't shown genuine romantic interest in me. I had gone on a few very awkward dates, but nothing of consequence. Then, Leo came along, out of the blue, in the most unlikely of circumstances. I thought he was God's idea for me.

If he was interested in me, there must be something special about him, right? Leo wasn't what I imagined for myself, being sixteen years older than me, divorced, and a biker. We didn't have a lot in common. He was also wounded; I could identify with that.

I was terrified when Leo first approached me and told me he had feelings for me. I analyzed my response and determined

I needed to face my fears. God must have brought him into my life to show me all the things I was scared of.

We started a long-distance relationship, where I could imagine Leo to be precisely the man I needed. Then, as things got more serious, he took my suggestion and came to Colorado and lived with my friends, so we could get to know each other better.

The person he was in real life didn't match up with the person I had imagined over phone and email conversations. I dismissed those thoughts and the sick feelings that would roll around in my stomach. He came all this way—that shows me I'm worth pursuing, just like Jesus seeks us—right?

The months went by, and I didn't find myself liking him more. I figured it wasn't about me; if God put him in my life, then God would give me the feelings I needed to have. In the meantime, with every struggle we had, I'd discover another fear or misconception I needed to face—so I was growing, right?

We traveled with some of my friends to a three-day church conference. After many prayers, watching how we both responded to the conference teachings, and some warnings from friends and strangers, I knew I had to step back.

I broached the subject with him. "God has been teaching me so much. The truth is I'm so worried all the time about making sure you're happy. All of my thoughts, every day, my decisions revolve around you. I'm afraid to say no—frightened you'll reject me or that I'm not good enough to be loved. I've felt like I owed you some massive debt of gratitude because you chose me despite my scars. I worry that I'm constantly disappointing you, and I can never measure up.

"From what I've learned, this is co-dependent behavior; it's unhealthy. I've behaved this way in other friendships and relationships too. God is showing me it's idolatry. I'm more concerned with what others think, including you, than what God thinks. So, we need to learn to relate in a healthy way. The only way we can do that is to step back and be friends."

He responded, "Well, if we're not going to be together, then we can't be friends." With that, he made preparations to go back home.

As he left, my eyes opened to the lies I believed about my value, purpose, and even what God would desire for me. God's love for me would not require that I sacrifice who I was or bind me up for someone else's freedom. He already provided the perfect sacrifice. Here is where I started to see a glimpse of how perfect His love is for me.

* * *

Where does fear begin? Not the fear that makes us escape danger or fight it off, but the fear that slowly builds itself around us until we are encapsulated and powerless. It all begins with a deception we believe is the truth. It was never a blatant lie like, "the sky is green, not blue." It seemed to be either ignorance, like "the earth is flat," or subtle, "you never do things right." When we believe lies as though they are truth and build our behaviors upon them, we are deceived. Until the truth comes along and disproves or dismantles the lie, we don't even know we live based on a fallacy.

That was me; I had built up a whole life on falsehoods that fed on mistrust.

Now there was a crack in the facade. That seam allowed a little light to come in, but I still couldn't see all that was false; the unease felt so typical. At the time, there was no way I could see the distortions for what they were. Seeing the little bit of light that appeared through the crack left me horrified by my stupidity and delusion.

To admit my weaknesses felt like I was setting myself up for my worst fear—to be unloved, rejected, alone. For a time, as I saw the reality of my deception, all I felt was shame and humiliation. Still, there is something about truth peeking through fiction. As I chose to believe veracity and confront the lies, no matter how backward it felt, the truth brought some surety and a measure of peace.

The lies and deception I had built my life upon came down to my view of God's love. There was no doubt in my mind He cherished me, for "the Bible tells me so." While growing up, my parents, grandparents, and so many others reminded me constantly of God's incredible love. It was like there was this block between what I knew and what I felt.

The best analogy I can think of is God is love. It is the essential ingredient that makes up

- who He is,

- what He does,

- how He reacts.

Love is His

- creation,

- justice,

- righteousness,

- discipline,

- salvation,

- provision,

- protection,

- mercy,

- grace,

- healing, and

- power.

The way He loves us, it's like turning on a fire-hose; it is strong and fierce; it has insurmountable power, gushing forward. Yet it's even more than that. This regard cannot be turned off or diminished. It is everlasting.

In my life, I hadn't always felt the force or saturation of this devotion. While His tenderness cannot be turned off, there can be kinks in the hose which prevent me from receiving all the affection God has for me. I was building my life on the lie that I needed to be perfect to be loved. I could allow myself to feel the satisfaction of God smiling upon me only if and after I had

- everything on my list checked off,

- a clean house,

- a washed car,

- taken care of the dog and the horse,

- done my homework,

- eaten the "right" things that day,

- exercised,

- sent thank you notes, and

- returned all my phone calls.

I felt as if He would be disappointed with me because of all the things I wasn't doing and accomplishing until everything was completed or brought into order. It was the same way inside my heart. I struggled with thoughts and feelings I hated. Words I didn't use or speak aloud screamed through my mind in my quiet moments. Pictures of things I knew were wrong flashed through my thoughts. I had dreams that took me places I never wanted to go. No matter how much order I attempted to bring to my life, I couldn't make my mind conform.

So, I prayed, repented, read my Bible, and tried harder to focus on being thankful. Still, the thoughts, feelings, insecurities, and fears would come back, proving to me I was incapable of controlling myself; I was failing, enforcing the idea that I wasn't worthy of being loved. There was no reason God should be proud of me. He knew what was in my heart and mind.

I saw myself weak, always missing the mark, uncertain, and scared. And I thought this was the way God saw me.

In His word, He said,

"...I have redeemed you; I have called you by name, you are mine." (Isaiah 43:1 ESV)

"I have loved you with an everlasting love; I have drawn you with unfailing kindness." (Jeremiah 31:3 NIV)

"I am fearfully and wonderfully made; your works are wonderful, I know that full well. My frame was not hidden from you when I was made in the secret place..." (Psalm 139:14-15 NIV)

"Now if we are children, then we are heirs-heirs of God and co-heirs with Christ..." (Romans 8:17 NIV)

"And if the Spirit of him who raised Jesus from the dead is living in you, he who raised Christ from the dead will also give life to your mortal bodies because of his Spirit who lives in you." (Romans 8:11 NIV)

"But you are a chosen people, a royal priesthood, a holy nation, God's special possession, that you may declare the praises of him who called you out of darkness into his wonderful light." (1 Peter 2:9 NIV)

It was tough to believe God meant all these words for me. But I recognized that if I took what I thought about myself and based my thoughts, actions, decisions, and future on them, I'd declare myself the truth speaker and God the liar. I was placing my thoughts above His.

God is not a man; He cannot lie. I was not wise enough to sit on the throne, and I was not living my life in the authority or the identity given to me as a child of God through Christ Jesus. We have an enemy; he is called the father of lies. He creates confusion and chaos wherever he goes with his favorite tool—fear. He hates God and what God loves. He knows when Jesus came to Earth, died for us, and raised himself again that Jesus created a bridge for us to relate directly to our creator, the Father.

This enemy knows God created us out of His love, and he knows how powerful God's charity is. Satan hates love, and he knows that where love is, there is great power. So, he begins his work to twist and distort our view of love from a very early age.

He wants us to see love as

- painful,

- something to be avoided,

- something we cannot attain,

- a thing to fear,

- controlling,

- abusive,

- judgmental, and

- hateful.

When we don't know what love truly is, we can't receive it or give it. And we are without power, freedom, and healing.

This enemy is the deceiver, helping us build a life on lies, a life filled with disillusionment, disappointment, and hopelessness. It sounds childishly simple in some ways. I wondered why it took me so long to get it. When I started understanding the enemy's goal was to separate me from God's love, I began to see more thoughts running through my head. They either reinforced God—His love, His thoughts toward me, His plan, and His place in my life—or they supported a lie causing me to doubt instead of trusting Him and live in fear of Him.

The best way I could know if my thoughts were truth or lies was to read God's word, to look for His love. He is a good and perfect Father, Savior, Merciful Judge, and Gracious Provider.

I began to sort out the jarringly harsh rebukes, endless rules, and hateful thoughts that drove me like a hard taskmaster, heaped expectations on myself, and wore me out. Even while I was doing "good" things, they were not from the voice of my Father.

Then, I got to choose—to which voice was I going to listen?

* * *

There are so many problems in our lives to figure out. We must not only pick at the fruit but dig deep, pluck it up by the whole root so it will not grow back. Then the fruit disappears, along with the plant that takes up space, casts a shadow, and houses undesirable critters.

That super deep root started with a seed. A seed, word, truth, or lie planted where it was fertile and ready to grow, watered, and nurtured by actions that supported the truth or the falsehood. In my life, I've had to approach many things by tracing the rotten fruit down to the root, examining what lie seeded the core, and then prying out the source and filling the space with the truth. I wonder if there are some people for whom the process is too painful, and the risk is too high, like it would completely break them—like opening Pandora's box or unsealing a contagion.

I contemplate times we plant seeds of truth all around a bitter root, then nurture and water those seeds of truth, so they grow big and strong enough that there's more truth than lie in the resulting fruit. This way, those strong, vigorous plants of truth choke out the bitter root, causing it and its fruit to die. However, that carries a risk; will the fruit of bitterness, lies, fear, or destruction cross-pollinate with the fruit of the spirit? Or, do we take solace in the fact that the fruit of the spirit cannot be defiled?

LOVING MYSELF

My injury and scars exposed me; they let me see myself and my heart. In it was something I couldn't ignore, imagine away, or fix. The vulnerability, nakedness, pain, discipline, and therapy required for my physical healing were necessary for my emotional and spiritual healing. I knew there was no way to hide from God because He could see what went on inside me.

The reality is, while I grew up as a Christian, I was broken before my accident burned away my identity and everything I knew about myself—before my life became a challenge few people face, and even fewer overcome.

As a teenager, I was already the hamster in the wheel, running and running to do the right thing; act, look, and react the right ways; make the right decisions. I ran to avoid pain, failure, consequences, and rejection. My scars weren't the cause of my self-hatred; they exposed it.

As a quiet person, I often developed friendships with outgoing, talkative people. They were full of life and fun, had opinions, knew what they wanted to do, and were creative and insistent. They liked me because I listened to them, was happy to follow their lead, and content to go where they wanted to go. If I didn't contradict them, it was easier for me. If I didn't come up with an idea they thought was stupid or weird, they would accept me, and I wouldn't be alone.

My friends often confided in me, telling me things about themselves they'd never told anyone, so I ended up understanding them better than most people. Once I knew their pains, weaknesses, and insecurities, I wanted to help them. When they called in the middle of the night, breaking down or getting themselves in over their head in some situation, I was happy they trusted me to relieve them in some way.

I was content to pay them back for being nice enough to befriend me. It looked as though some of these friends were controlling and manipulating me to my family and long-time friends. My response, when questioned, was that nobody else understood my friend the way I did. In time, I became worn out by the impositions. I told myself that saying "no" was not loving them unconditionally.

My reward for my efforts was the complete "honesty" of these types of friends. They told me what others thought of me—something we all wonder, but nobody discloses. The "truths" I learned helped me shape myself into the type of person nobody could dislike or reject.

I worked my way up the ladder, becoming a more trusted friend and integral part of their lives, always hoping to secure the position of being wholly accepted and loved for who I was. And safe.

But there was a reality constantly chasing me. No matter how much I did or gave, or how indispensable and trusted I was, one misstep, mistake, or glimpse of my authentic self on the inside would knock that ladder out from under me. There, lying on the ground, I would either be discarded or have to start over again—working my way back up.

As such, I lived without boundaries. After all, boundaries were selfish (or so I thought). In my quest for the life granted me to help others, I could not be closed off. But I was getting worn down. The opinions and thoughts disclosed by my "honest" friends followed me everywhere I went. They dictated my actions regardless of their physical presence.

I had no idea, but I ruled my life by intimidation. I allowed others to frighten me into making me do what they wanted. This timidity caused me to be quiet, comply, just go with the flow, and not trust myself, my thoughts, or my opinions.

I was mad at myself all the time because I couldn't follow my own rules. I thought of boundaries as walls—and "good Christians" did not have erect barriers. I loved people; I wanted to show them how much. To say "no" isn't fun; it doesn't feel good. The lie is that most folks don't like people who tell them "no." Wanting to belong, I strove not to be a person who said "no."

My family has unconditional love for each other. While we may not agree with each other or understand one another all the time—we love each other no matter what. This means no matter what decisions we make or where our life goes, our connection doesn't change. We don't lose our position in the family, we aren't banished or rejected, and we don't stop talking to each other. There's no way I understood the full scope of unconditional love in my family. Remember, I was living based on what I perceived their expectations of me to be—but I always wanted to be someone who loves others unconditionally, to be "Charity," God's perfect love.

I thought unconditional love meant never saying "no." In attempting to use that guideline, I was losing myself.

"Teacher, which is the greatest commandment in the Law?" Jesus replied: "'Love the Lord your God with all your heart and with all your soul and with all your mind.' This is the first and greatest commandment. And the second is like it: 'Love your neighbor as yourself.'" (Matthew 22:36-39 NIV)

Looking at my relationships and the position I had placed myself in, it was becoming apparent I didn't recognize my worth. In my mind, it was okay for people to use me if it helped them. Somehow, that gave my life purpose. I directly correlated sacrifice with love. If I wasn't sacrificing myself—my likes, desires, and needs—I wasn't loving God or others.

Every action I made in an attempt to love others felt like a sacrifice, slowly chipping away at my identity. I look back now and realize I loved everyone that way. When they didn't see my sacrifice or love as enough for them, my solution was to chip away more of myself and offer that to them as a temporary consolation. Why was I sacrificing myself for their benefit when Jesus already did that? In essence, I was implying Christ's sacrifice wasn't enough. How could I do that? His is the only sacrifice that's enough.

I was getting in the middle, trying to shield them from God's discipline or the consequences of their actions, because I didn't want those I loved to experience any level of discomfort or pain. After all, I knew how that felt. But my thinking was twisted. I thought "carrying one another's burdens" meant taking other's problems as my own and trying to fix them.

These people weren't trying to heal; they just wanted to feel good. I valued their freedom more than they did, worked on getting it for them, and they were happy to let me.

"Do nothing out of selfish ambition or vain conceit. Rather, in humility value others above yourselves, not looking to your own interests but each of you to the interests of the others." (Philippians 2:3-4 NIV)

I took that piece of Scripture literally and out of context. Failing to recognize Christ, Himself—who laid down His life for us—still had boundaries. He gave Himself freely, instead of letting others decide for Him. Though He served those around Him, He was not a slave to their whims. He humbled Himself, but He never forgot who He was or who His Father was.

It began to dawn on me:

- If I couldn't love myself the way Christ did, then I couldn't see He valued me enough to save my eternal life.

- If I couldn't believe I was who God said I was, then I couldn't receive His charity for me.

- And if I couldn't receive His charity for me, then I denied God the ability to love me infinitely.

- Therefore, I was unable to love Him and others fully.

- Subsequently, I could not even follow the first commandment—to love Him with all my heart, soul, and mind.

- It takes receiving His pure and perfect love to have it and give back to Him.

- In not receiving His love, I can't cherish myself.

- And, in not valuing myself, I can't adore God or respect others.

It was a vicious cycle.

RESTORING MY SELF LOVE

I had to choose to agree with what God thought of me,
     instead of what I thought
          of myself;
I had to step back
     and see what He delighted in.
As I observed my love for my little brother and sister,
     the way
          my heart would go pitter-patter,
               as they walked into the room,
          how their little hands felt in mine,
          I swooned when they chose me to play with,

or ask me questions.
I loved them
    before they were ever able to do anything at all,
    even when they were utterly dependent and
    needy.
I adored
    watching while they formed their
        personalities,
        humor,
        strengths,
        passions, and
        seeing them enjoy the world around them.
Through them,
    I better understood how God saw me.
    I started to love what He saw.

* * *

When I can't see how lovable I am, I won't recognize the many ways others cherish me; I can't believe their regard is genuine; I don't know the favor bestowed on me. This blindness puts me in the position of always longing, fighting, and striving for something I already have—but think I don't. It's another deception—believing a lie as though it is accurate and basing my actions on a lie.

* * *

Boundaries are a necessary part of connecting with others. I needed to set them as an essential step to valuing my needs. A boundary does not have to be a wall; it can be a fence that contains what is mine and protects me from predators. A structure also tells others that I'll grant entry only with permission. I didn't realize people feel safer with limits. Boundaries make it clear how far someone can go before they cross over into another territory.

But to establish clarity, one must say, "no, you cannot cross this line," and this is where "tough love" comes into play. I never wanted to enforce "tough love;" I wanted to be "happy, loving, and feel good."

Boundaries also give stability for growth. Without a trellis, a vine would spread across the ground, leaving its fruit to rot and its branches vulnerable to destruction.

Without "tough love," I didn't allow the people I loved to see the truth and the boundaries that would contribute to our relationship's growth. I was endangering them, allowing them to live in a delusion. Eventually, someone who didn't care about them would tell them the truth—without love—and it might crush them.

Because I lived a life with no established boundaries and full of fear, I couldn't suddenly change my circumstances and relieve my pain. Instead, I had to begin the long, arduous task of dismantling fear in my life—a task easier said than done. I was afraid of things for a reason; I was pretty confident they could destroy me. Facing my fears felt like walking into the lion's den.

In some cases, my worries built walls to protect me, and I needed to destroy them. Doing so left me feeling vulnerable and uncertain. Creating healthy boundaries where none existed takes time and effort. I had to determine where those boundary lines needed to be, then gather the material and expend the effort to establish them.

Some couldn't believe I put up a boundary; so, they would test it, throw a fit, and try to dismantle it. I would have to stand and reinforce it, all while doubting myself, feeling selfish, and wanting to give up, yet remain strong and defending my boundary line.

In each task—dismantling fear and rebuilding boundaries—I needed to, somehow, be able to get ahold of the love and protection God's word promised me. If I didn't, I would surely go through all of that effort only to discover I had put new walls of fear in place. And I would have to repeat the process and reinstall my boundaries.

* * *

Due to my broken translations of Scripture, God's character, and sense of Christian duty, I struggled with guilt and shame even while I acknowledged, owned, and worked through the mess I had made in my relationships and life.

Self-condemnation was a familiar companion, constantly reminding me of the pain I had caused others. And how easy it would be to give up, leaving more casualties in my wake.

"For if you forgive other people when they sin against you, your heavenly Father will also forgive you. But if you do not forgive others their sins, your Father will not forgive your sins." (Matthew 6:14-15 NIV)

For some reason, it was pretty easy for me to forgive others—especially when I saw the infringement was unintentional, done due to their own wounds, or simply out of ignorance. I had great compassion for the fact we all had bad days and made mistakes. I genuinely believed we needed a safe place for us to grow and learn.

We can't expect perfection; we're kids, students of the kingdom, and need the space to practice our lessons until the choices become natural.

When I refused to forgive, I gave a past misdeed space, time, and physical and emotional energy in my present life. Although the past can't be undone, we can learn from it and heal from past wounds. We can wish it never happened, but we can't change the past. Unforgiveness mires us in the past. For me, remaining stuck muddies the way I go about today—how I treat others and even how I approach life.

My problem wasn't forgiving others; it was forgiving myself.

Whether it was the fact I hit the brakes and changed the course of my life and my family members' lives or it was the comments I made that had hurt others—a long list of "should-haves" and "only-ifs" rotated through my mind daily. As I attempted to believe I am who God said I was, I had to wade through all those condemning, unforgiving thoughts.

Why could I forgive others so quickly but not forgive myself? I was holding myself to an impossible standard—one I didn't require of others. This was not the way I would treat my sister or a friend. So, if I were to love myself at least as much as I love them, I needed to forgive myself. If I don't, God will not forgive me.

Ultimately, I couldn't accept that He had totally and completely forgiven me and appreciate the gift of that freedom when I declared myself the judge and sentenced myself to penance. Instead, I rejected Christ's sacrifice for me, defining myself as something less than God's very own. In practice, I distanced myself from His love as well as my ability to love Him, myself, and others.

> I WAS HOLDING MYSELF TO AN IMPOSSIBLE STANDARD—ONE I DIDN'T REQUIRE OF OTHERS.

However, the truth can

- build me up,

- restore peace and joy,

- remind me of its unending love,

- tell me that God chose me,

- reinforce the notion I am worthwhile and not a waste of time,

- whisper how strong I am, how wonderfully He created me,

- tell me I have value and purpose,

- remind me how I love my family and friends, and

- make me willing to give everything I have for them and to them.

And that kind of love and truth comes from God within me and me in Him. It shows me my creativity and passion, inspiration and motivation, drive and intelligence, humor, wit, and charm—the things that make me who I am—have nothing to do with my accident or scars.

It declares that my circumstances and experiences contribute to my knowledge, wisdom, self-awareness, and how I react to situations and pressure. Love and truth have helped draw out my perseverance and endurance and contributed to the character only they can create.

It states that there are plans for my life; I wasn't a random accident, and a fire didn't destroy my destiny.

It reiterates that I am dearly loved.

The truth equips me to face another day and declare it a victory. These truths are woven into the fabric of my being, and they help me love myself and receive love from others. Finally, these truths give me confidence, security, and courage.

10

ACCEPTANCE

Dave Roever stood on the stage of a large high school auditorium and spoke to the teenage audience. There were about 300 students present on a Friday evening. His story was captivating. I sat near the back, up on the balcony with my friends. They had heard Dave's story before and invited me to come along. I was fifteen years old.

Tears flowed down my face as I listened to him replay the events that left him disfigured. He talked about his service in the Vietnam War. He had been nicknamed "Preacher Boy." Duty and a love for his country had put Dave on a riverboat in enemy territory.

Snipers fired on him and his companions. He grabbed a grenade, pulled the pin, and aimed to throw, just as an enemy bullet hit the grenade. It blew up while still in his hand and threw him into the water.

Dave talked about his time in the hospital, his fear of losing his wife, feelings of hopelessness, and suicidal thoughts. He'd lighten the mood and play the piano by "ear." Then we discovered he removed his prosthetic ear and used it to push the keys on the keyboard.

It was the first time I had ever seen someone who was severely burned. That night I became aware that even through the most significant pain, this man loved Jesus. And regardless of what he went through, he chose life—a good, whole life. It was possible. Unbeknownst to me, I would require the knowledge I had gained that night just a little over a year later. When I woke up in a hospital bed, burned beyond recognition, I knew deep down this was something I could live through, and I could have a good life.

Years later, God brought Dave Roever across my path again. I was able to share the seeds he sowed in that auditorium, ones I had applied to my life. I thanked him for the hope he brought to a room full of teenagers. This connection began a friendship that allowed me to work with his organization and see firsthand the fruit God can produce through a life and testimony offered to God for His use.

* * *

When facing loss, the final stage of grief is labeled "acceptance." Honestly, I'm not sure I fully "accepted" my injury until I stopped having reconstructive surgeries. In seven years, I had twenty-some-odd surgeries. In every surgery, there were four to six procedures done.

I had implants put into my chin and cheek, multiple nose surgeries, and numerous surgeries on my neck, eyelids, and hairline. Surgeons worked on my right hand to make it functional. The list goes on to include facelifts, liposuction, scar renovation, and laser surgery. After every operation, I secretly hoped I would somehow defy the odds and return to my former self.

My body was weary of the surgeries—it wasn't healing as quickly, and there were more complications. So I "took a break." It ended up being permanent. I soon discovered there was such freedom in not planning surgeries for every school holiday. I hadn't realized how the surgeries were keeping me from moving forward with my life; they were keeping me in a perpetual state of healing. Every surgery carried with it the sober reminder of why I had to go through it, bringing my losses to the forefront of my mind and restarting my grief cycle.

When I stopped having surgeries, the past no longer appeared in my present every three months. Then, I was able to start dreaming about the future and fully living. Soon, I began seizing opportunities presented to me. When asked to help staff summer mission trips overseas, I said yes. This commitment had me sharing bathrooms with twenty girls, sleeping on church floors, dancing all over the world, sharing my testimony on the streets—to the homeless, in rehab centers, nursing homes, parks, churches, schools, and more. Now I could let go of myself, really start helping others, and see the lengths God would go to heal hearts.

I already had taken small steps toward living, taking riding lessons, and purchasing a horse. I loved my art classes and made sure I was taking one every semester. I started a non-profit but eventually dissolved it. I spent time traveling to see family and friends. And I said "yes" when asked to share my story at churches or schools.

While it had been many years since my accident, it wasn't until I began to love myself that I was truly able to accept who I was. I don't mean approving of the scars—although there were times I got weary of wearing them. It meant accepting that

- God created me for a purpose; He gave me gifts and talents, and it was my responsibility to steward those;

- the role of leadership when I'd rather do what others asked, and do it well;

- my strengths and allowing God to be strong in my weakness—even though I hated being weak;

- my beauty and believing in it;

- my love of myself; and loving others as well.

No longer would everything be better if I just looked "normal" again. Now life was better because I knew I had value, even if I had nothing to give. I had accepted the "me" who was missing fingers and covered in scars. I acknowledged this "me" was good. The wounds were not going to hold me back from my destiny. Maybe, they were even part of it.

Perhaps God had allowed this tragedy in my life because He could trust me with the weight of carrying scars while showing His grace and spreading His love. Conceivably, He wanted people to remember His miraculous power when they saw me.

IDENTITY

It's interesting how we pigeonhole people. We can see a person working every day at the grocery store while in the checkout line. In our minds, we label or define that person as a checkout clerk. Then one day, in a snippet of conversation, we learn she has children at home—our definition just got bigger; she's a mom now too.

Another day, she is taking longer than usual to ring up your groceries. You look at her face—she looks worried and tired. You ask her what's wrong, and she informs you her husband is in the hospital with heart problems. Her world is even more involved now in your mind; she is no longer just the checkout clerk at the grocery store. She is a working mom and wife with real-life problems, wondering how she will juggle her children, job, husband's health, bills, and house.

Identity is a crazy thing. We see people in one light, and we imagine we know them—who they are, how they act, and what they feel and think. But what about our identity? Our identity is who we are on the inside—what we believe, how we feel, how we respond, our sense of humor, our fears, our passions. All of this is what makes us individual; it's how we base our life.

Some people live their life around their family name—as it makes them feel valued and significant. That name is to be protected, honored, and upheld. Others live their life around an occupation. What about the person consumed with being a doctor? Everything they read, watch, or study has to do with the medical field. They rarely go out with friends; they set aside family because they need to study; make their grades; get the scholarship, an internship, then eventually the job. Fast forward; now they have their own family, and they treat their spouse, children, and friends as patients. They base every decision they make on whether or not it would benefit their career.

What about pro-athletes, actors, musicians? It's easy for their passions and careers to be their identity. It's tricky when we take on a name, career, or talent as our identity. This focus begs the question: What happens when someone slanders our name? What happens when our career is over? What happens when someone else outdoes us? How do we retain our identity? Do we then become non-persons?

Some would apply a new label like "failure" or "loser" to their identity and self-worth, having wrapped up their value in a consumable commodity. Once these people no longer have a monetary value or use, they deem themselves garbage. Others have significant roadblocks or obstacles and don't throw themselves away. What's the difference? Maybe their identity is not based on what they do.

We tend to label people, categorize them, and define their world. We're quick to pull out labels like

- poor,
- disabled,
- abused,
- divorced,

- sketchy,

- smart,

- beautiful,

- talented.

We have many applicable labels, some on race, culture, religion, or family dynamics. We see people, label them, and think we have them all figured out.

Enter a life-changing, disabling trauma. When we are badly hurt, either emotionally or physically, we see everything through the lens of that event. For instance, if you are hospitalized due to a severe burn, that injury affects your whole life. All of a sudden, the scars, pain, and trauma have wrapped themselves around every aspect of your life—your relationships, the way you react, and the decisions you make.

The physical scars may create new fears. They may cause you to see yourself differently so that you limit yourself and change how you accomplish things. They impact everything—your vacation plans, vocational choices, social life, even the way you dress. For a while, the only way you see the path ahead is through that lens. That's okay for a time; that may even be necessary for healing until the trauma threatens to become your identity—the thing that sets you apart, that makes you unique. It threatens to label you. How do you repel the stigma wanting to attach itself to you?

Recognize that your identity, the person you are, is not what happened to you. Yes, your life experiences help form who you are; but one life event cannot define you. You are much more than that.

There is only one thing we should base our whole lives on. Not our relationships, jobs, financial decisions, what we wear,

> YES, YOUR LIFE EXPERIENCES HELP FORM WHO YOU ARE; BUT ONE LIFE EVENT CANNOT DEFINE YOU.

what we eat or drink, where we go, or what we do with our time and energy. The one thing should be the label that marks us; that label is "God's child." This is the safest place to be. With this tied to our identity, we will

- discover a future and a hope for us, regardless of what we've been through;

- find healing for our broken hearts and a fitting way to love others;

- embrace deliverance from our fears;

- discern the many things to be grateful for; and

- recognize many others are going through things much harder than we could imagine.

As God's children, we can ask Him to work in the situations of life that overwhelm us, and He'll hear our prayer, give us wisdom, and help those others who are hurting. There is room for the impossible, the miraculous when we use His name. Then we realize all the other labels we could have chosen would have confined us to a particular set of demands. But, to live under God's banner gives us great freedom—to be all He created us to be, beyond what we could ask or imagine.

My strength, wisdom, comfort, peace, trust, and safe place, are all in Him—not because I did anything to deserve this but because when He created me, He put a heart inside me that would want to know Him more. He gave me the ability to have any faith at all, the strength to choose Him, and the tenacity to seek and find Him.

As I know Him more—I start to comprehend who I am even more. No longer is my identity about my scars, talents, job, financial position, social standing, or ability to be "good"—a good daughter, granddaughter, sister, aunt, cousin, friend, wife, daughter-in-law, homemaker, artist, or even author.

Just like a victim's identity is in their injury, every aspect of their life revolves around their lack. When I tie my identity to good things, like being an overcomer, every part of my life revolves around my performance.

When my identity is in anything other than Jesus, I determine my value by my ability. A good or bad day, mistakes, failures, successes, and accomplishments become the measuring stick declaring my value. It changes up and down with whatever perception I have of myself.

In facing my fears, replacing lies with truth, learning to love myself, and learning to accept my circumstances, I get to see more and more of who I am, how I'm gifted, the way God works through me, and how He works in me. As faith replaces fear and truth pushes back the lies, and as I receive more of God's love, I cement my security, confidence, hope, and assurance in the fact that I am God's child.

It seems to me that American teenagers spend more on beauty products and clothes than previous generations did at their age. According to the recent reports from the CDC, the suicide rate for teens has been on the rise. The teenage pregnancy rate in the U.S. is still "substantially higher than other western industrialized nations." Teenagers seem to do anything to be called "beautiful" and to belong. When they feel they've missed the mark, they plummet to the depths of self-loathing.

I have always been one of those girls who liked clothes, makeup, and styled hair. I always wanted to look good. As a student, I rifled through my closet and my sisters' closets, trying to put together cute and trendy outfits. My mother, who knew very little about fashion, would tell me how nice I looked as I headed out the door to go to school. I would leave the house feeling confident it would be a good day because I had the right outfit.

The minute I stepped onto campus, that confidence disappeared. All of a sudden, a strand of hair insisted on going its own way. I would see other girls and immediately consider my clothes substandard. My peers looked me up and down, labeling me as a "wannabe," or so I thought anyway. No matter what I did, I could not make my acne clear up, or my hair behave; I could not magically change my second-hand clothes into brand-name ones.

I was sure I was not beautiful, not even pretty. The facts reinforced my view of myself: I didn't have a boyfriend, and I wasn't popular. Lies fed my stories: only cute girls had boyfriends, and only pretty girls were popular. Yet, each day I started again—I selected my clothes, did my hair and makeup, and hoped that day, I would be beautiful.

As a shy, quiet girl, I classified myself as having low self-esteem. If I had thought higher of myself, I would have classified myself as arrogant, boastful, or vain, and I was taught those were sins.

Of course, the media played into my self-esteem issues. Images from TV, magazines, catalogs, book covers, billboards—pictures of beautiful, perfect girls constantly barraged my consciousness. I wanted to be like them, to have their figure, muscle tone, complexion, straight white teeth, perfect hair, flawless makeup, beautiful clothes—picture-perfect lives. Today, I see those images, and just like most women, a part of me still longs for that kind of beauty.

I'm not the only girl who searches for beauty, thinking somehow, it's the key to ultimate happiness. Now it's an epidemic. Women worldwide are inflicting pain and misery upon themselves in extreme efforts to become what they or society deem "beautiful."

The more I'm around women and young ladies, the more I'm amazed at the number of them who find themselves less than enough. Many stunning, intelligent, and very gifted ladies are stuck in their insecurities. They have no concept of their beauty, value, or worth.

When I'm not enough in my own eyes, then I can never be enough in another's eyes, and I can't be enough in God's eyes—so why try? I might as well settle for less. Otherwise, I'd spend all my focus and energy striving to look like the ideal images plastered all over the magazine racks, TV, movies, and advertisements.

Everywhere we turn, it seems, society implies women need to

- be a perfect size two,

- exercise three to five times a week,

- eat healthy food,

- drink lots of water,

- work full-time (outside the home),

- wear beautiful clothes,

- don flawless make-up,

- keep an impeccable home,

- be the ideal mom with perfect children,

- be the stunning wife with a fabulous husband.

Otherwise, there is something very wrong with us. It pains me to see even those who seem to have it all together are also insecure and trying to change themselves to feel valuable and worthy to be loved.

It's incredible the depth to which these lies have rooted concerning our value and identity. We have a society of anorexic teenagers, compulsive young adults consuming health foods of all sorts, working out for hours a day, and condemning themselves for each gram of carbs they consume. We have forty-plus-year-olds lining up for plastic surgery or weight loss therapy. Each generation sets their minds on the flesh, comparing and competing, which leads to death in the end.

"The mind governed by the flesh is death, but the mind governed by the Spirit is life and peace." (Romans 8:6 NIV)

We spend so much time trying to look proper, normal, healthy, strong, and independent. When we tie our identity to something superficial and temporary, it leaves little time to invest in relationships, family, each other, and things that last for eternity.

* * *

While sitting in the tire store waiting area one Saturday morning, I watched a line of customers all doing the same thing I was—trying to get our cars cared for in the small window of business hours available on the weekend.

My wait was quite long, although I was just getting two new tires. What made it seem longer was the country music playing over the sound system. I've lived quite a few years in Texas, where country music is unavoidable, and I have to admit my toe does start tapping all on its own when it plays. But feelings of self-pity seem to come with country music that I don't want to have—especially in public.

I remember working in my dad's shop after we moved to Colorado. Every day, for hours upon hours, country music played on the radio. I don't know why my dad listens to country music now. When we were kids, we listened to varying genres—The Eagles, Pink Floyd, Led Zeppelin, Neil Diamond, The Mamas and The Papas, The Beach Boys. How in the world did his music preference change so much?

After only moments of the country station being on in my dad's shop, I would find myself sitting in my office, trying to hold back the tears. There were days I was more resilient, and the tears never came; however, many days, I could not restrain them.

I think my reaction wasn't because of the number of songs filled with sob stories or that the station played the same ten songs repeatedly, but because the songs are so real. Country artists have a way of painting a picture of a simple, joyful life, where true love lasts forever; songs with genuine feelings of blissful pleasure and deep pain. They make a listener want that kind of life. Who doesn't wish for nights lying in the grass looking up at the stars, long drives on country roads, days sitting on the front porch, or evenings riding off into the sunset?

Who doesn't yearn to find themselves at the end of life, married to their long-time true love? What girl doesn't want to be the prettiest girl ever in somebody else's eyes? Or for him to write songs about her?

And there's the problem. Immediately when I heard the strum of a guitar, sitting in the tire shop, I started comparing. I contemplated the reality that I would never be the most beautiful girl everyone stares at when she walks into a room. Okay, maybe they do stare at me but for a different reason. My life didn't go in the direction of marrying my high school sweetheart, and in my years of waiting for my "Mr. Right," I felt true love, for me, had been short-lived, if it had existed at all.

Instead, I face a bigger reality; when I think of myself as not beautiful, as many women do, I know I can't fix it. I can't cover up my scars, and my worst day cannot be neatly tucked away into the past. I can't change the effects of a split-second decision. I can't lose weight, get a makeover, or buy some new clothes, and voila—be beautiful. That's the pit comparison can get me stuck in.

Comparison makes me start focusing on what

- I don't have,
- I'll never have,

- hasn't come,
- has been lost.

Comparison highlights my reality. It brings jealousy, self-hatred, condemnation, and unfulfilled imagination. Comparison takes me down a slippery slope—one that is hard to climb back up. I stop seeing the joy in everyday life. Instead of feeling satisfaction in my accomplishments, I see only the flaws. I reject my best attempt because comparison reminds me of the imperfections and lack and causes me to view my efforts as a waste.

With comparison as my sidekick, I will never celebrate the joy of true success; contrast constantly belittles the best a person has to give. Observing differences is the lens through which I view my life; nothing is good enough. Nothing can bring me that true sense of joy, gratitude, fulfillment, peace, and contentment I deeply desire. Then, I begin to look for a source to blame my discontent.

First, I see those who have the life I view as perfect—those with a happy marriage, beautiful family, gargantuan house, expensive vehicle, connection to their true love—and I fertilize the soil for the seed of jealousy to grow.

My pride may grow and spill over into how I treat them, accentuating their lack so I can feel better about myself. Comparison causes me to keep searching for the key to unlocking my happiness. While I want to make my inaction mean something about my friends, the truth is, they will still be happy—with or without me, so I can't blame them.

I could blame Hollywood and the media for my discontent as its influence infiltrates my life with visions of perfect bodies, hair, and teeth; how can I help but compare? One movie after another portrays love conquering all, the underdog winning, and beauty overcoming chaos. The heroine loves the beast despite his manner. Why can't my life (or my thighs) look like that?

Then I step back and do a reality check; those movies are fiction. Those size-two actresses are (technically) professional athletes who spend hours every day in the gym and count every calorie. After all, it is a job requirement to have that perfectly toned (airbrushed) body. How can I blame them for my discontent as I sit on the sofa eating a(nother) brownie?

I could examine my life as far back as I remember and find misinterpretations and pain in my childhood—things I built upon to create instability in my foundation. I could blame my parents, siblings, classmates, or friends. Truthfully though, what I do with wrongs done to me and around me, real or imagined, are my own choices; the consequences are mine.

I could blame the accident that took my face, identity, and years of my life. I'd like to blame my scars, to establish them as the culprit of lack in my life. However, if I start to make my wounds the source, I have to ask, *how can I blame a natural result of healed wounds?* How can I blame something for "ruining" my life when it's opened my eyes and my heart?

The scars have been part of showing me who I am and given me opportunities I would never have otherwise had. So, while in comparison mode, I would like to make my appearance the enemy. Yet, while they make shopping a challenge and first impressions awkward, they aren't the source of my discontent.

The only common factor left is me; I became my worst enemy. I am the one withholding my ideal life. I am the source of my discontent. When I compare, I measure my life or somebody else's and determine the winner according to a frequently changing scale, never quite balanced. I make imagination the goal and fail to enjoy the substance and the journey through my life. All the blessings around me go unnoticed; instead, my focus is on the lack.

> I AM THE ONE WITHHOLDING MY IDEAL LIFE. I AM THE SOURCE OF MY DISCONTENT.

The truth is, even if I did somehow reach that imaginary goal, comparison would keep me from enjoying the prize. Then, any gratitude would dissipate, and pride would refuel resentment, leaving me more miserable as I step back into the cycle of comparison.

So, I have to stop comparing myself to others. If I must continue, I should contrast who I am today with who I was a year ago, five years ago, twenty years ago. Then, I would see growth, healing, wisdom, and an increase of love, joy, and peace.

This type of self-comparison creates a natural outflow of thankfulness for the good life I have. Suppose I see something important to me diminishing over time. In that case, this perspective provides me with an opportunity for self-reflection—to see why my "something" is less than it was before. And it allows me to make a change.

I also make sure I keep the country music to a minimum; my life is much happier that way.

* * *

"Will someone marry me?" This plea for assurance was a post on Facebook made by a girl no more than fourteen years old who was severely burned in a house fire. She was trying to be silly. It was an inside joke between her and a friend, but not all her friends saw it that way. One comment stuck out to me, probably because I have heard it many times before. "It'll be someone extraordinary, someone who can see the beauty that's inside of you."

Honestly, I know what people are trying to say: internal beauty has more value than external, and that's true. However, it's also true that those who see "beyond the surface," who love us for who we really are, are special people. Regardless of what we look like, don't we all want someone who loves us despite our appearances?

I'm not sure I particularly want to wait for "Mr. X-ray vision"—who only sees the inside—or for someone who's blind. Instead, I want others to see what I have learned to see—there is beauty in the scars.

BEAUTY IN THE SCARS

Scars
  be unashamed
  not despised;
  Marks of triumph.
  Trauma overcome.
Little girl,
  burned,
  exposed to
    incredible pain
    and loss,
  choose
    a life lived fully
      despite your injury.
You still
  have years to recover,
Adjust to your
  new body,
    which you will eventually love,
Warrior girl,
  embrace the struggles,
  choose to fight through them,
  love yourself.
See all of your beauty,
  your worth,
  unconfined,
  undefined by traditional thoughts,
  inside as well as out;
Write your own song.

ACCEPTANCE

Beauty is
fleeting,
skin deep,
not the supreme goal.
Face challenges head-on,
Do not avoid:
places we deem ugly,
things we consider untouchable,
areas we shun,
View them from a different angle;
they can be beautiful.
If we only take a moment to look:
There is beauty in the scars.

And believe, once again, in God's word.

"He has made everything beautiful in its time..." (Ecclesiastes 3:11 NIV)

I have to believe He didn't make me beautiful once, for it to be snatched away early in my life and then become unattainable. Instead, I have faith in the miracle-working, all-creative, heavenly Father who loves me.

"And we know that in all things God works for the good of those who love him, who have been called according to his purpose." (Romans 8:28)

"For we are God's masterpiece. He has created us anew in Christ Jesus, so we can do the good things he planned for us long ago." (Ephesians 2:10 NLT)

Redefine beauty to encompass the masterpiece God made each of us into today—as He continually works all things for good. God can make beauty from ashes; He redeems life from the pit. He delights in us and finds joy in us.

"...to bestow on them a crown of beauty instead of ashes..."
(Isaiah 61:3 NIV)

"He will take great delight in you; in his love he will no longer rebuke you, but will rejoice over you with singing."
(Zephaniah 3:17 NIV)

My identity is in God; I take His word over me as the truth and value what He does. I can stop comparing my life to those with different gifts, callings, and purposes. I choose to remain in the position He placed me in and have begun to see the beauty all around and within me. I love myself and others as He loves. I recognize I am not alone, and I can walk with His grace, step into my destiny, and call others into theirs. That's the ongoing work of an overcomer.

PART III

BEYOND THRIVING

11

THE WORK OF SUFFERING

It sounds crazy, but when we embrace the pain and suffering of life's hard times, we do great work. Running to Jesus in my pain helped me better understand His suffering on my behalf. Being met by a loving Savior gently highlighted that it wasn't all about me. He understood and showed me He had much better plans than those I could see.

CHANGES

My conversation with Jesus was crystal clear. It was about sixteen years after my accident. I had experienced freedom and healing at that point in my life, but I felt out-of-sorts. I was confident and secure in my identity, having served in ministry for several years.

But things were changing in my life. I knew it was time to go to new places. The ministry I had been working with for several years was in my comfort zone. I had learned and grown a lot during the plethora of adventures with the other people who served together. We all knew how to work together like a well-oiled machine. I belonged, I added value to the team, and my friends loved me. It would have been easy to live my happily ever after with them.

My future was not clear to me, but I started to feel God nudging me to other places He wanted me to go and things He wanted me to learn. It was exciting and scary at the same time.

You know, with significant life changes, several things need to happen.

First, you have to prepare for the change.

1. Examine the change.

2. Assess what's going to be required.

3. Draft a plan.

4. Implement your plan.

For example, if the change is moving, you have to find out where you are going, get everything ready on that end, pack up your current location, and, of course, move.

Another example requiring preparation is during a change in seasons. We may have to adjust our clothing preferences. So we look through our wardrobe (or packed boxes) and determine which clothes would be appropriate to wear given the impending change. Much like my childhood days, long before we had cell phones or weather apps, we lived in Texas—where it can be as hot as seventy degrees or as cold as thirty degrees on any February day. Of course, I always seemed to have it backward and would be wearing short sleeves on a cold day and bundling up on warmer days.

Whatever the change is, there's a period when things are messy and out of order, leaving us exposed and vulnerable. I can be a little slow working through change, like when I haven't quite registered that the season has changed. Or when God's in the process of moving me to a new place.

That year, I had all sorts of feelings I hadn't experienced in a while. I felt hopeless but didn't know why. Things were going well, and I had found my rhythm. However, I still had unanswered prayers, and I was getting tired of waiting for God's timing—which seemed to take forever sometimes. I was considering giving up on Him and trying to do things on my own.

In the depths of my hopelessness, I remember praying. "I know the soldiers beat you to a pulp and ripped the skin from your body by the lashes you endured; they forced you to carry your cross after suffering extreme abuse. I can only imagine the agony of being nailed to and hung from that cross; the pain must have been unbearable. Please don't consider me ungrateful; I recognize your sacrifice. But Jesus, your pain on the cross lasted one day; mine spreads out over many years. I'm tired of wearing scars and never getting a reprieve from them."

Wow! I sure was feeling sorry for myself! I know. What *audacity* to say such a thing to Jesus. It's a wonder God didn't strike me down right then and there! But do you know what I heard, deep down, in the depths of my soul? "Charity, your pain was big; it was the result of an accident." An ever so gentle voice reminded me.

"I knew my pain was coming, for the joy set before me—I endured it." (Hebrews 12:2)

He continued, "I knew what the result would be. The real torture was the fact that people I loved caused my pain. These people had no idea what they were doing as they mocked and abused me, as they spewed hatred and anger at my gift."

"Today, I still endure the pain of mockery. The pain of being misunderstood. The pain of rejection for giving the ultimate gift. I'm not diminishing your pain, Charity. Even though our suffering was different, I understand your pain."

Boy, was I humbled! And I came to love Jesus more. Somewhere, in that conversation—in the gentle, kind rebuke—I better understood Jesus' pain and recognized I could never contemplate the true depths of His sacrifice. He came to Earth a humble, compassionate man, serving as He taught about the kingdom and a relationship with His Father. Displaying grace and strength in the face of opposition, He suffered for us so we could know His Father the way He did. He ensured our eternal security, giving us the greatest gift—one we could never earn or deserve. He defeated death and ascended to His rightful place in heaven. He sent us the gift of the Holy Spirit, the comforter, the revealer. Still today, He continues to give, preparing a place for us, for our joy and delight.

> *"Dear friends, do not be surprised at the fiery ordeal that has come on you to test you, as though something strange were happening to you. But rejoice inasmuch as you participate in the sufferings of Christ, so that you may be overjoyed when his glory is revealed." (I Peter 1:12-13)*

He became my safe place.

INTIMACY WITH JESUS

After experiencing pain repeatedly, I came out the other side stronger, healthier, and more whole. While I didn't want to invite suffering into my life, the fruit of it was priceless. Suffering showed me the truth. It showed me how great God was in my weakness. The misery showed me I could endure unimaginable things, and I was stronger than I ever thought. It also allowed me to foster compassion for others.

Little things, material things no longer mattered; I placed a much higher value on those I loved and worked to ensure my relationships remained intact. Over time, I better equipped myself to receive God's love and truth. As a result, I was able to deepen my love for myself and others.

In every trial I experienced—suffering the result of my burn injuries, losing loved ones, enduring wrongs done to me by others, or facing the consequences of my own foolish choices—I got to choose my answers to several questions. Would I

- allow this trial to do its thorough work in me?

- delve deep for treasures in the trials, to discover places God showed me His goodness and grace?

- offer my weaknesses and let Him strengthen me?

- permit this trial to bring me closer to Jesus?

- or would I sanction this trial to pull me away from God?

"I want to know Christ—yes, to know the power of his resurrection and participation in his sufferings..." (Philippians 3:10 NIV)

When I identify with Jesus in my suffering, take Him my pain and my heartache, being honest with Him about how I feel, and put forth my fears—He understands.

He shows me:

- He, too, carries scars put there by hatred and false accusation rather than an accident.

- His wounds, chosen to be worn for eternity.

- He knows how it feels to be mocked, ridiculed, and misunderstood.

- He acknowledges the pain of being separated from His Father.

- He comprehends the feeling of losing someone who He loves.

- He grasps how overcoming hard things for the sake of those He loves can hurt.

In this place, my love for Jesus grows. Suffering produces intimacy with Him. That is where I start to glimpse how much He has given on my behalf—for my freedom.

PURPOSE IN PAIN

Maybe when we cry out to God to know Him more, love him more, allow Him into our lives, and ask him to be more involved in our lives, we invite Him to use the tools necessary to answer our prayers. Suffering is one of these tools, similar to how a surgeon has to inflict pain to cause healing; He recognizes that discomfort will help us get to know Him better. Isaiah 53:10 (NIV) says, *"Yet it was the Lord's will to crush Him and cause Him to suffer..."* It pleased Him because He knew the result.

As we give our lives to God and forsake our own ways of doing things, we can experience a level of suffering. I don't imagine God sitting up in heaven, cheering as we ache. Instead, I believe He weeps with joy that we would lay down our self-preservation and embrace adversity that comes with knowing Him better. Our hardship produces sweet fruit. He gives back so much in the economy of His kingdom when we entrust our suffering to Him.

In my situation, I was unable to avoid pain. It resulted from the doctors and nurses protecting my body from life-threatening infections as they cleaned my wounds daily. Life-improving surgeries created more wounds to heal. Physical therapy allowed me to regain use of my limbs and independence. I could not run and hide from pain; it was unavoidable if I wanted to get better. Not only did I have to allow it, but I also had to invite it into my life. The longer I avoided it, the more I feared it, the longer it took to get through it and bring about its purpose in my life.

> OUR HARDSHIP PRODUCES SWEET FRUIT.

I got to choose: would I allow this pain to make me stronger, or would I allow it to defeat me? When I don't let suffering do its thorough work in my life, I let the adversity win. Pain wins when I walk in fear, run from, or try to fight it. These actions often injure me more in the process.

When perseverance proves too difficult, I give up, accusing God or blaming Him, perhaps even becoming offended with Him for my suffering; it creates a prime place to cultivate that bitter root in my life. All of that results in not allowing the fruit of the Holy Spirit to grow in my life. It does not allow me to establish His character through His presence in my circumstances. Just as God prepares me to care for the good things: purpose, calling, and abundance, He also primes me to handle the adversity that will come my way.

God knows what lies ahead for my good; He rejoices in giving me incredible blessings. However, He is also cognizant of what the enemy plots against me. He is just as invested in building me up with the ability to withstand enemy forces as He is in training me to rule and reign with Christ.

Training to withstand the enemy hurts and may require learning to endure pain for years. I am strong enough to fight the same battle repeatedly until the enemy shows his weakness, and I take him down. During the fight, I may become dirty. I might have to live in uncomfortable situations for an extended time, separated from my loved ones. It may feel like being repeatedly beaten. While this training would be difficult, and I might want to give up, I have to fight through it or give myself willingly over to the enemy.

The only absolute freedom is to continue training until the day of victory. Honestly, it sounds kind of twisted. Is it possible that

- without pain, there would be no need for healing?

- without suffering, there would be no need for a miracle?

- without injustice, there would be no need for a judge?

- without sin, there would be no need for a savior?

God knew what separation from Him would create:

- I would endure hardship; it would hurt, and I would need relief.

- I would also need to learn to shield the enemy's fiery darts to survive his attacks.

- There would be pain and suffering. Yet in His love, He made a way for me, for all of us. His purpose is not to keep me from pain—He didn't save His own Son from pain—but to make a pathway through suffering to victory; to put the enemy under my feet. He gave me the only lasting strategy enabling me to be the final champion—Himself.

"Therefore, since Christ suffered in his body, arm yourselves also with the same attitude, because whoever suffers in the body is done with sin. As a result, they do not live the rest of their earthly lives for evil human desires, but rather for the will of God." (I Peter 4:1-2 NIV)

Somehow, in the suffering, I learned to trust God with all my heart. I wanted to avoid and run from the pain and tried to shield my loved ones from it. But challenges are the doorway to strength and authority. Trials are essential to know Jesus better, receive more of His love, and do the work He commissioned us to do.

He cemented His goodness into me. Regardless of how things appear, I know, beyond a shadow of a doubt, that He is for me, and He is with me always. Therein lies the peace that surpasses all understanding. When I put all of my trust in Him and find my safety in Him, it keeps me from harm.

12

WHAT IS IT TO THRIVE?

When you sit enthroned under the shadow of Shaddai, you are hidden in the strength of God Most High. He's the hope that holds me and the Stronghold to shelter me, the only God for me, and my great confidence.

He will rescue you from every hidden trap of the enemy, and he will protect you from false accusation and any deadly curse. His massive arms are wrapped around you, protecting you. You can run under his covering of majesty and hide. His arms of faithfulness are a shield keeping you from harm.

God sends angels with special orders to protect you wherever you go, defending you from all harm.

For here is what the Lord has spoken to me: "Because you have delighted in me as my great lover, I will greatly protect you. I will set you in a high place, safe and secure before my face. I will answer your cry for help every time you pray, and you will find and feel my presence even in your time of pressure and trouble. I will be your glorious hero and give you a feast. You will be satisfied with a full life and with all that

I do for you. For you will enjoy the fullness of my salvation!"
(Psalms 91:1-4, 11, 14-16 TPT)

BEING INTENTIONAL

I grew up reading the King James Version (KJV) of the Bible. The scriptures I memorized for Sunday School and many of the songs we sang during worship were based on that version.

My mother was a brilliant woman; she loved to learn and study. Being a new Christian when I was born, she taught us how to use a concordance and tried to help us translate the variation of words like *thus, thee,* and *thou* as we read our Bible stories.

Today, I love the fact I can plug a partial verse into my search engine, and it immediately shows me what I'm looking for—in all the versions. Life is so much easier!

I believe the New International Version (NIV) of the Bible was too new during my childhood, so people didn't use it widely. Many of the churches I attended frowned upon any other version than good old King James. I can understand why.

As a youth, I tried to develop daily Bible reading habits. Honestly, it felt like most of my Bible reading was a puzzle to work out—a lot like deciphering Shakespeare in high school. I spent more time translating and less time absorbing the meaning.

When I was a young adult and reattempted developing daily Bible reading habits, I still found myself frustrated and stumped. I didn't see the lessons others seemed to find in their Bibles. When others proclaimed "a scripture stood out to them," I couldn't relate. But I wanted to. I truly wanted to see God's character as I read the stories. As I experienced more and more freedom, I aspired to know God more, and the best way to do this was to read His Word. After all, is that not why He gave it to us?

I understood the fact everything was about a relationship with God. Not works or a list of dos and don'ts—measuring my righteousness according to how well I'm able to follow the rules. That was precisely the reason Jesus came; because none of us can achieve the standard required to be in the presence of God Himself on our own.

I wanted to know the Word, have it "hidden in my heart," and see it "living and active" in my life. An internal battle raged as I listened to pastoral teachings pointing out the "evils" of reading other versions of the Bible. So, I continued in my struggle—only getting drops when I needed a long drink—never developing a practical Bible study regime.

Then, I heard a sermon. The pastor said, "You crave what you develop an appetite for." He went on to explain if you ate cookies and candy all day instead of fruit, that's what you would crave. If you drank sodas all day, you would crave soda instead of water. If you filled your hours with meaningless things, you wouldn't desire education.

What I surmised was that if there were things in our lives we knew were good for us or would improve our lives, we must develop an appetite for them. To crave exercise, we must exercise regularly, pushing through the temptation to give up; eventually, we will want it. Disclaimer—this hasn't worked for me so well.

Likewise, to crave the Word of God in our lives, we must be intentional about reading the Word every day. For a while, it may feel like you're slogging your way through—going through the motions—but one day, you'll see it becomes something you desire.

It seems to me when God created man in His image, He made someone He could relate to, walk, talk, and laugh with. He could pour out love on His children, who had the capacity and free will to love Him in return.

When I discover someone I want to know better, I try to spend as much time with them as I can: getting to learn their history, what makes them tick, what they think, how they feel, and their opinions—so I can understand them.

Regarding my relationship with God, I realized if I would declare Him first in my life—if I were going to follow His commands, I needed to carve out time for Him every day. My actions required me to line up with my declaration.

> *"...what does the LORD your God ask of you but to fear the LORD your God, to walk in obedience to him, to love him, to serve the LORD your God with all your heart and with all your soul, and to observe the LORD'S commands and decrees that I am giving you today for your own good?" (Deuteronomy 10:12-13 NIV)*

I needed to be intentional. At first, it was clumsy as I started with a devotional to help guide my quiet time. While I acknowledged the concerns about venturing from the King James Version (KJV) of the Bible, I decided to find a version to study that I could understand and had notes to explain scripture further. For a while, I compared versions, side-by-side, with my KJV.

I prayed the Holy Spirit would help me understand the scriptures and apply them to my real life. I started out small. I had coffee with Jesus for fifteen minutes every day with a mug in hand, reading a devotional with scripture. Behold! One day, a scripture stood out to me; I saw a more profound meaning and how it applied to what I was going through at the time.

Finally, I understood God speaks all the languages and knows how to communicate with His children worldwide. The Holy Spirit can reveal the truth of the Word of God in any translation of the Bible.

God opened my eyes, and my hunger to know Him grew. I started wanting to read through the Bible, and I formulated a plan to do so. Dusting off the study skills my mother had taught me, I began to look up scriptures pertaining to whatever

I was working through at the time. I wrote down what I learned, journaling what the Holy Spirit revealed to me. And I started craving more time to learn; I sought to know God even more. The more I read, the better I could identify the lies in my life—because I understood God's character better.

> *"But if from there you seek the Lord your God, you will find him if you seek him with all your heart and with all your soul." (Deuteronomy 4:29 NIV)*

It's incredible to me that the God of the universe allowed us to find Him. He patiently waits for us to show us how things work and why. It's a two-sided relationship fueled by absolute love.

Now, I need that time—not because it's my "Christian duty," but because it grounds me. I find myself longing to hear God's voice, please Him, and bring Him joy—because I love Him. As I know more about Him and witness His love toward us, I love Him even more.

When life throws me curve balls and disrupts my quiet times, I find myself feeling lost, less secure, and full of doubt. God quickly sets all of this right when I make time for Him. And then, I can observe more of His work, kindness, and goodness—in every detail of my life.

THANKFULNESS

If I approach life from my perspective—God came to Earth to serve me:

- He died for me;
- He will deliver me;
- He will grant my heart's desires.

When I struggle to find peace, joy, and contentment in my current situation, my thankfulness dwindles to the most basic, elementary level. While all of the statements above are true, they highlight how I approach the God of the universe—putting my perceived needs above His great plan.

On the other hand, when I approach life through His perspective—everything comes from Him:

- His sacrifice,

- His love,

- His freedom,

- His mercy,

- His grace,

- His favor,

- His delight,

- His choice,

- His abundance—

  - given to me freely—

    - for His glory,

    - for His purposes,

Then thankfulness comes easy, and joy follows. The reality is that He

- is massive, and I am dust,

- chooses to partner with me of all people,

- wants to communicate with me,

- desires to be in every part of my life,

- understands my ins and outs,

- knows my desires, and

- has a plan for my good.

All of this humbles me and gives me every reason to have a thankful heart. It's easy for me to view my life through the lens of lack, focusing only on what is not here yet, waiting for the fulfillment of promises, and seeing only what I've lost or will never have. The truth is there is so much God has given me; it far outweighs my perceived lack (or even true lack) at any given moment.

> *"Therefore, since we are receiving a kingdom that cannot be shaken, let us be thankful, and so worship God acceptably with reverence and awe," (Hebrews 12:28 NIV)*

* * *

My sister shared a story about her two oldest kiddos; Eliana was eleven years old, and Mikey was ten years old. Mikey was going through a stage where nothing was good enough; he always complained about something. He was angry and frustrated most of the time and was not fun to live with. His mama tried to encourage him to be thankful during these times, but her words fell on deaf ears.

One day, Eliana, a quiet-natured child, piped up and relayed to Mikey, "There was a time when I felt the exact same way. When I was angry, frustrated, and finding things to complain about, I started choosing to be thankful instead. I looked for things to be thankful for. At first, it was hard, but I had to practice gratitude. As I practiced, it got easier."

My sister recalled watching her daughter choose to be thankful. She remembered, at first, Eliana's smile and thankfulness seemed forced. Now, her girl has a genuine, joyful, sweet attitude. Mikey may not have completely understood what Eliana was communicating that day, but I believe that seeds of gratitude were planted in his life. Today he is a content and creative teenager who enjoys serving those he loves and is a pleasure to know.

* * *

"But godliness with contentment is great gain." (1 Timothy 6:6 NIV)

Contentment is a battle; once I obtain it, I have to fight to retain it. Discontent is familiar to me, yet, I hate feeling it because I'm thankful for so much. Nevertheless, discontent weasels its way in so subtly, blinding me to the wealth of provision around me, robbing me of my grateful heart, and leading me down a path of entitlement. When I find myself wandering down the familiar path of discontent, I need to apply the same problem-solving skills I use when dealing with change.

First, I trace the discontent back and look for the fear fueling it. Often, I dread not having or being enough; I'll be forgotten or suffer pain. I lock in that anxiety by comparing my lack to others' abundance. I justify my discontent and begin complaining.

> CONTENTMENT IS A BATTLE; ONCE I OBTAIN IT, I HAVE TO FIGHT TO RETAIN IT.

Second, I have to ask myself, do I trust God? Most of the time, when I find myself dissatisfied, I have narrowed my view of God's faithfulness toward me. I have failed, again, to see the daily miracles provided on my behalf. I've reattempted to solve my perceived lack with my abilities—which are limited.

As I begin to slide down the slippery slope of discontent, the best way to find a foothold and climb my way out is remembering. The same applies when complaining, comparing, and coveting start banding together in my heart and mind. I remember all God has done to care for me, deliver me, heal me, and make a way for me. I stand firm on those truths. Then, my discontent dissolves and makes space for gratitude. I also make a concerted effort to stop thinking about what I don't have. This focus frees up a lot of my time.

As I look at what I *do* have, I become more impressed with how good my life is and more grateful for how well God is taking care of me. It becomes apparent again that He knows what I need much better than I do. I don't deserve this favor, but I'm thankful for it. In light of the miracle of today, I see something else forming in my life: joy.

GOD'S LOVE

A phrase comes in like a vapor, a whisper, and then takes shape and form; it reminds me, "God chose me, and He wants me for Himself."

"For he chose us in him before the creation of the world to be holy and blameless in his sight. In love he predestined us for adoption to sonship through Jesus Christ, in accordance with his pleasure and will—" (Ephesians 1:4-5 NIV)

I'm tempted to simply nod my head and agree, "Yes, Jesus loves me." But I stop and ponder what that means because I know somewhere down deep, in that simple statement, is something I need that will give me more than momentary comfort.

"For I am convinced that neither death nor life, neither angels nor demons, neither the present nor the future, nor any powers, neither height nor depth, nor anything else in all creation, will be able to separate us from the love of God that is in Christ Jesus our Lord." (Romans 8:38-39)

HE CHOOSES ME

God of the universe,
    God our Creator,
        Protector,
            Father,
                Savior,
                    and Friend
who knows me inside out and upside down,
who's aware of
    my flaws,
        my insecurities,
            my unbelief,
                my stubbornness,
                    and my selfishness.
He still chooses me
    even today,
        even when I feel like a mess.
He still loves me
    even when
        I am angry,
        or offended;
        and my thoughts are not
            nice,
                holy,
                    pure,
                        good,
                            true,
                                or lovely.
He doesn't abandon me;
    even as I push against Him,
        aware of why I feel the way I do.

He pursues me,
    not wanting to share me,
        keeping all of me for Himself.

He offers me
    far more than any human being can give me.
He loves me
    far beyond how a human could love me.
He strives to be my source of
    comfort,
        strength,
            encouragement,
                joy,
                    love,
                        and life.
He explains because I've received the gift His Son—His
Love—gave
    I am good enough for Him.
Why would I want anything less?
God's love is the foundation
    to everything:
        His mercy,
        His justice,
        His judgment,
        His discipline,
        His healing,
        His provision,
        His salvation,
        His creation,
    based on incredible, unconditional, unwavering, unchang-
ing, love,
    is available to me.
The more intentional I am in relating to Him,
    the more I see Him.
He sees it all,
    where I am today in my journey,
    where life is taking me.
He considers the temporary and the eternal.
He chooses me.

* * *

So many times, I've asked God for more of His love. As if He's holding back, withholding something from me, I need to do what He has asked of me, which is to love and serve others.

God's love, His provision, His care are unlimited. Sometimes I forget that truth. Often, I think I've received my portion, so I have to wait until I do something good for God to refill my cup.

> *"so that Christ may dwell in your hearts through your faith. And may you, having been [deeply] rooted and [securely] grounded in love, be fully capable of comprehending with all the saints (God's people) the width and length and height and depth of His love [fully experiencing that amazing, endless love]; and [that you may come] to know [practically, through personal experience] the love of Christ which far surpasses [mere] knowledge [without experience], that you may be filled up [throughout your being] to all the fullness of God [so that you may have the richest experience of God's presence in your lives, completely filled and flooded with God Himself]." (Ephesians 3:17-19 AMP)*

His love is like a waterfall or a fire hose—more than we can contain, a constant rush, never stopping. Sometimes I feel like it's merely a drip, taste, or tease, and I beg for more. However, the backfill is already there.

What if the fears and lies I believe or the way I measure my performance stems from the amount of love I allow myself to receive from God? Then, it's me stopping access; I'm the regulator adjusting the flow from the hose according to my perceptions. I'm slowing my allotment to a drip, rationing it as if it's something that may run out. How that must hurt God's heart.

WHAT IS IT TO THRIVE?

When I realize my self-limiting beliefs and receive my position as His well-loved child, the impossible happens. I shake off shame, guilt, and condemnation and build healthy relationships. My compassion for others moves me to action, where I embrace my destiny, building His kingdom—forgiven, free, His.

YOUR LOVE

Your love goes on and on and on and on and on,
Without end,
Without measure,
Without limit,
Without partiality.

No situation,
No circumstance,
No sin,
Brokenness,
Anger,
Offense,
Hatred,
Can stop it.

Confusion,
Misunderstanding,
Distraction,
Do not redirect it.

Laziness,
Passivity,
Aloofness,
Unbelief,
Lack of faith,
Hurt,
Do not diminish it.

Lies,
Deception,
Bitterness,
Offense,
Aggressiveness,
Evil,
Do not squelch it.

Nothing can silence it;
Nothing can remove it;
It goes on and on and on and on and on for me.

And me, I am to have that love for others.
Love that goes on and on and on and on...
Whether they agree with me or not,
Whether or not I'm loved in return,
Whether or not I'm understood,
Or valued,
Or even liked.

My love for others should not look like
Fear,
Control,
Worry,
Manipulation.

It shouldn't be silenced when
They don't do things the way I do them,
Or the way I want them to,
When others don't see what I see
Or believe the same way
Love that goes on and on and on and on...
It does not have an off switch.

WHAT IS IT TO THRIVE?

It is not regulated
According to behavior,
Or favor,
Or influence,
Or beauty,
Or lack thereof,
Or wealth,
Or hunger,
Or sickness,
Or disease,
Or trauma.

It goes on and on and on and on...

13
HOPE AND WHOLENESS

HOPE FOR OTHERS—A GIFT TO GOD

A couple of years ago, my grandparents celebrated their seventieth wedding anniversary. Seventy years! Can you imagine? They did something right. They are thoroughly devoted to each other. When I grow up, I want to be just like my grandparents. They have been such an example of love, and they show it by loving others as well. I am grateful they have cherished each other in front of us.

My grandparents are best friends. They have always done things together. When Grandpa led my dad's and uncles' Boy Scout troops, Grandma packed the lunches and made sure they all had their sleeping bags. From weekend water-skiing on the lake to family road trips and moves across the country, Grandpa and Grandpa have fully shared their lives. They volunteer together, work together, play games, and partake in hobbies they both enjoy; they are a united team.

"Work now, play later" was my grandpa's mantra. He retired early. Their family has always been their biggest love. We know this because all eight of us grandchildren are confident we are their favorite.

They spent time with us as we grew up. I have fond memories of Grandma working alongside us as she taught us how to do hospital corners when making beds and as she had us slice the carrots to go with the dinner Grandpa was grilling. If we all worked together to get the job done quickly, we knew we could swim, play cards, or have another lesson in crocheting.

One of the greatest lessons I learned from my grandparents is that, while work is imperative and playing is important, loving others well by spending time together is essential.

DON'T HOLD BACK

My grandparents went the extra mile to care for others, literally. They traveled thousands of miles at their own expense to share their hard-earned recreational time with family members who lived far away. Every year they plotted their routes, determining who they were going to visit or who most needed their help.

Wherever they were, they were fully present, offering their skills, company, and hearts. They tilled gardens, refinished furniture, towed vehicles, packed up homes, settled estates, changed diapers, bandaged wounds, washed countless loads of laundry, and babysat dogs. I don't recall ever hearing my grandparents say "no" if there was any possible way they could help. Their love for others was selfless.

"It's just the right thing to do," Grandpa simply stated. I have heard stories and watched as my grandparents did what was right, even when it was hard.

They saved when money was tight, offered sandwiches and water to lonely travelers, spoke up for those who were wronged, and went out of their way to help someone broken down on the side of the road.

So today, when I work extra hours to do the job right, when I clean up a mess I didn't make, when I restrain myself from cutting corners, or when I walk my shopping cart all the way to the designated area, I know part of the reason I'm trustworthy is that I "do the right thing."

As we grew up, our grandparents worked hard to treat us fairly. They never wanted one grandchild to feel less loved than the other. They always supported us, encouraged us, and worried about us, but they were determined to be there for us.

When they did not understand why we did the things we did or disagreed with our choices, they never withheld their love—that was unconditional. Regardless of how crazy our schemes seemed, they generously showed their support because, in their mind, that was simply the right thing to do when you loved others well.

ALWAYS SAY, "I LOVE YOU"

Every time we saw each other, every time we parted, and every conversation ended with, "I love you." There was absolutely no doubt in our minds our grandparents loved us. They sent birthday cards with letters and thoughtful Christmas gifts. They made room for us in their homes and were always there with a hug, pop in the fridge, or a ride from the airport.

They constantly declared their love in ways large and small because they knew life could be unexpectedly cut short. They also knew that our greatest treasures on Earth are each other, so they loved others well. And do you know what? I've never met anybody who didn't love them!

"This is my commandment that you love one another…that your joy may be full." (John 15:12 NIV)

As I focus on loving others, helping where I can, speaking encouraging words, or offering a smile, the concerns I have, the sadness I may be feeling, or the struggles that keep rotating to the front of my thoughts diminish.

There is power in giving, whether it's finances, time, energy, gifts, talents, or prayers; God takes the little bit I have to give in the simple ways I offer, and He composes it into something far beyond what I can imagine.

The Bible provides countless scriptures about giving and helping others, whether it's about taking care of widows and orphans, the boy with his two fishes and a loaf of bread, or about the greatest gift a Father can give—His very own Son. God did not create our lives to experience it alone or serve only our own needs and wants.

"…Freely you have received; freely give." (Matthew 10:8 NIV)

He's the best at giving, and He loves it when I, His child, give. I'm doing as my Father does. I believe there is a type of gift that God especially loves for us. It's not something He requires, but when given to Him as an offering, as a gift of adoration or worship—His heart goes pitter-patter. That gift is my pain. When I take my pain and offer it and all its associations—memories, wounding, and lessons learned—to

Him, I imagine God is incredibly pleased. The gift is much sweeter when He does not require it from me.

> *"...the God of all comfort, who comforts us in all our troubles, so that we can comfort those in any trouble with the comfort we ourselves receive from God. For just as we share abundantly in the sufferings of Christ, so also our comfort abounds through Christ." (2 Corinthians 1:3-6)*

* * *

> *"Blessed is the man whose strength is in thee; in whose heart are the ways of them. Who passing through the valley of Baca make it a well; the rain also filleth the pools. They go from strength to strength, every one of them in Zion appeareth before God." (Psalm 84:5-6)*

I learned from a sermon Dave Roever gave that the *valley of Baca* translates to the valley of tears. To me, this is a dark place where there's often confusion, torment, and pain. Here, it can be tempting to give up entirely, to lose myself in the valley where the pain is tremendous and the darkness endless. Sometimes the long journey is too hard, and I value myself too little to make it worth the effort to move forward, keep fighting, and prevail.

GRAB A SHOVEL AND DIG

When I'm going through those times in life that just hurt, whether it's along the pathway of going to new places and starting new things or somewhere along the path of loss, I need to take the time to stop and reflect. Even when all I can do is weep, I'm not to rush, running through the valley as quickly as possible to get to the other side.

When I take time to seek God and put words to the journey, to mark it; then, I am "digging a well." If I stop and reflect on the circumstances, a different strength comes forth. I realize my current pain and the associated lessons can bring refreshment and hope. Looking through the tears, I see there may still be something I can give in the midst of them.

I recognize the battle isn't singularly for my own healing, overcoming, eternity, or victory, but for future generations and those assigned a similar journey. Then, there becomes a glimmer of purpose that lays a pathway for love and leaning toward others. In "digging a well," I am marking a milestone in the valley of tears. God brings rain to fill the well of living water, refreshing, healing, life. The milestone tells the next person walking through the same place that they aren't the only one wandering along—someone else has been on this path. There is hope, rest, and comfort along the way.

And I am blessed. Somehow, in this process, I feel the strength to get through my current circumstances and the challenges to come. Because when I take the time to dig a well, I can also stop to see the wells already dug by others. I get to drink deep the living water that has filled them. It gives me strength, courage, and hope to continue.

PEACE—MY RESTING PLACE

"You will keep in perfect and constant peace the one whose mind is steadfast [that is, committed and focused on You—in both inclination and character], because he trusts and takes refuge in You [with hope and confident expectation]." (Isaiah 26:3 AMP)

To me, wholeness goes beyond surviving, beyond overcoming, even beyond thriving. It is freedom, living in truth, living loved and living to love. I look back at the years when I experienced torment. Ugly thoughts, unresolved issues, and impossible situations filled my mind. Lies orbited around me, following me everywhere I went, like buzzards circling their prey. Fear was my constant companion.

Then, God's word broke in. It was a lamp at my feet and lit my pathway to freedom. There I found peace. It wasn't a passing peace ebbing and flowing according to my moods or emotions. Nor was it rising and falling with the balance of my bank account. The light didn't shine brighter or dimmer, according to my relationships. God's word became my resting place.

Peace is the place I run to when uncertainties arise in my life. It's a place that took a lot of work to establish, one I fight passionately to keep. It has become the gauge with which I measure my position relative to God and others. Peace is a treasure to keep close.

When I'm tempted to follow things that want to steer me away from God's highest, when the voice of tranquility quiets and starts to feel further away, or when its comfort is alluding me, leaving me chilly and feeling uncovered, I run back to peace.

> PEACE IS THE PLACE I RUN TO WHEN UNCERTAINTIES ARISE IN MY LIFE.

When circumstances cause friendships to become confusing and relationships to get messy, I find myself fighting for peace. Real, lasting stillness is not battling to be right or insisting on winning but based on truth, trust, and love. Peace doesn't come from sweeping things under the rug or at the cost of losing myself; it comes from speaking the truth in love and bringing God the healer into the situation. Peace comes from trusting Him when

- I don't understand.

- I can't see what He is doing.

- The diagnosis is terminal.

- My loved ones are lost.

- I get bad news.

- He feels quiet and far away.

Serenity comes from trusting He is the same, yesterday, today, and tomorrow. He is still for me and not against me and working on my behalf; He is still good; He still loves me and is my only hope.

"This is what the Sovereign LORD, the Holy One of Israel, says: 'In repentance and rest is your salvation, in quietness and trust is your strength...'" (Isaiah 30:15 NIV)

To me, peace is an integral part of thriving, living abundantly, and beyond my circumstances. It's the result of abiding—of living in God and He in me. Peace is the safe place, the shelter, the place I come home as God's child.

"Blessed are the peacemakers, for they will be called children of God." (Matthew 5:9 NIV)

MY ANCHOR—HOPE

"Therefore, since we have been justified through faith, we have peace with God through our Lord Jesus Christ, through whom we have gained access by faith into this grace in which we now stand.

And we boast in the hope of the glory of God.

Not only so, but we also glory in our sufferings, because we know that suffering produces perseverance; perseverance, character; and character, hope.

And hope does not put us to shame, because God's love has been poured out into our hearts through the Holy Spirit, who has been given to us." (Romans 5:1-5 NIV)

Hope is one of those words I tend to throw around loosely. Sometimes I wrap hope in unbelief and treat it like a wish in a fairytale. It can be a pat answer—an attempt at comfort when words elude me. Or it can be the anchor for my faith.

Real hope, the kind that holds me steadfast and gives me light when everything around me seems dark, is not easy to come by. Scripture tells us the pathway to that kind of hope is through suffering. Not just a little discomfort, but an affliction that tends to stick around long enough or happen often enough to require perseverance.

Perseverance is the ability to keep standing, even when

- it's difficult,
- it's not popular,
- others don't agree,
- it hurts,
- I want to run and hide or just give in,
- I don't know how long the battle, illness, or struggle will last.

Then character comes along; it develops along the way. I look back and find myself stronger. I recognize I want to make the right choices, even when the right decisions are tough—because the result will be worth it. Character allows me to confirm I'm trustworthy, dependable, and faithful. I discover that love moves me to action more than fear, and I dig deeper for truth instead of blindly following the lies.

Hope and trust (co-mingled) are a daily necessity and spearhead my faith.

"Now faith is the substance of things hoped for, the evidence of things not seen." (Hebrews 11:1 NKJV)

The critical ingredient to hope is faith, and a little measure of faith can move a mountain.

"And hope does not put us to shame, because God's love has been poured out into our hearts through the Holy Spirit, who has been given to us." (Romans 5:5 NIV)

God's love, faith, and hope take me far beyond surviving:

- allowing me to see the miracles all around me;

- permitting me to be confident in who He created me to be;

- filling my life with purpose, compassion, and value;

- providing a foundation to believe in the impossible and to share it with others;

- giving me the courage to move forward, fulfill my calling, and invite others.

While there are struggles I still face daily, things I cannot begin to understand, and heartbreaks I must still face, hope gives me the security to know that whatever comes my way, God will get me through it. Not only will He get me through it, but He will also make beauty out of ashes (Isaiah 61:3). Resting in that knowledge, knowing I don't have to work through anything in my life on my own, is a relief, as is knowing I am completely loved and treasured—no matter what.

"Now to him who is able to do immeasurably more than all we ask or imagine, according to his power that is at work within us, to him be glory in the church and in Christ Jesus throughout all generations, for ever and ever! Amen." (Ephesians 3:20 NIV)

I look back and consider the prayers and dreams of my seventeen-year-old self. There was no way I could have possibly imagined the life I would have. My perspective was so small. I see now that God has done and is doing much more in my life than I ever could have thought to pray for. He has taken me places, let me meet people, and walked me through experiences that never entered my mind as a possibility.

The greatest gifts He has given me—beyond my freedom and wholeness—have been in my relationships. He has provided so many amazing people—family and friends—who love me unconditionally, help, care, listen, share, and provide outstanding examples of God's incredible family. They are instruments of His love and grace, constantly teaching me more about who He is and displaying His light through them.

That's what living a life beyond thriving is to me. It's a life connected to what I need most, for whatever comes my way—a life connected to God. My life is worshipping Him, loving Him, and continually working to know Him more. It recognizes His love as the principle upon which I am saved, healed, rescued, restored, and redeemed.

"May the God of hope fill you with all joy and peace as you trust in him, so that you may overflow with hope by the power of the Holy Spirit." (Romans 15:13 NIV)

EPILOGUE

by Christina Freeland Duran

I was a freshman in high school when Charity, Roseanna, and Nikki were in the car accident. At the time, I wouldn't have called our lives "easy." I had all the teenage angst and drama any other typical teenager can remember. (And I still wonder why people say ridiculous things like, "Oh, to be a teenager again!") But the most challenging aspects of life I remember from before the accident were our regular moving, changing schools, making and readjusting to new groups of friends, learning new cultures, and trying to understand all the weird phrases regularly used by Louisiana folk.

The time since the accident has now been a much larger portion of my life than the time before, and there is no question each of us has gone through hard things since that year. Yet, the accident remains a pivotal point in my life.

The greatest legacy our mama left us was introducing us to an eternal savior. She taught us, sang to us, and prayed in front of us to Jesus for as long as any of us remember. He was her hope, her solid rock, her redeemer, and her faithful God. He transformed her life and gave her hope when she had felt hopeless. Each of us knows the times in our lives when we hit a place where we came to the end of ourselves. Mama gave us the gift of knowing who to turn to when we had nowhere else to go.

During and after the car accident, we got to see the faithfulness of God in action. We were heartbroken, distressed, anxious, and terrified—beyond our abilities to meet any of the problems in front of us. And God drew near and carried us through, every step of the way.

There has not been a significant trial that has happened since the accident in which I have forgotten the faithfulness of the Lord to carry us through. This is not only the legacy Mama left to us; it is the legacy Charity lives. She expresses that faithfulness in God through every aspect of this book.

That faithful God freely offered His Son for you too, dear reader. He is eager, able, and powerful enough to meet you in your need as well.

Where are we now?

Grandma and Grandpa Freeland are still living in Arizona, and we treasure each ounce of time and wisdom we get with and from them.

Papa is in Colorado, happily adjusting to what normal people would call "retirement."

Charity is in Colorado, thriving in the community there—always cheerfully serving and bringing her gifts and talents to the table to help make others' lives better.

Roseanna is in Mississippi, surrounded by people she loves and who love her. She is indispensable in her profession.

I'm happily married in California with a large number of kids running around. If they stay still long enough, I'll try to count them for you.

Clay is in Colorado, married to a lovely gal, with four kids and seven grandkids at last count.

Laura is paving her way through Texas with a Texas-sized heart, love for truth, and passion for life.

And the faithfulness of God ties us together, carrying us through.

FINAL NOTE FROM CHARITY

One of the best gifts God has given me is my family. They have loved, supported, laughed, cried, watched, waited, dreamed, and listened to me every step of the way. They are my teachers, my best friends, and my whole heart.

I am amazed by the individuals they are and how God works in and through them. I wanted you to see a bit of what I get to witness in them every day; that's why I asked Roseanna to write the prologue and Christina to write the epilogue. Without their voices speaking in my life, I would not have my own.

I pray this book has shown you how deeply connected God is to our suffering:

- how good He is in the midst of it,

- how faithful He is to walk with us,

- how capable He is to heal us,

- how compassionate He is to our weaknesses,

- and how miraculously great His love is for each of us.

CHAPTER DISCUSSION QUESTIONS

CHAPTER ONE: THE FACTS

1. What is the most significant pain you've ever experienced?

2. Aside from yourself, who else suffered from your pain?

3. How did you respond to your pain?

Going Deeper

4. Have you experienced a shift in your priorities? What things are important now that may not have been as important before?

5. What miracles did you experience amid your tragedy?

CHAPTER TWO: CHOICES

1. What kinds of choices are in your control?

2. In what ways are you choosing life?

3. How are your negative choices affecting you and those who love you?

Going Deeper

4. What are the words/thoughts you spend most of your time on?

5. What is God saying about you through His Word? Do you believe it?

CHAPTER THREE: HEALING

1. Do you feel like you are all alone, and no one else can understand your pain?

2. Who can you talk to?

3. What does community mean to you?

Going Deeper

4. Are there things you aren't trusting to God?

5. Who are the people you learn from the most?

CHAPTER FOUR: GRIEVING LOSSES

1. What have you lost that you haven't grieved?

2. How do you view pain? Is it something you avoid at all costs?

3. What has pain produced in your life?

Going Deeper

4. Are there wounds you've ignored and left untreated?

5. Can you see things to be thankful for as a result of the pain you've gone through?

CHAPTER FIVE: FAITH

1. Where is your faith? Have you committed your life to Jesus?

2. Do you believe God is on your side and He is for you?

3. What are some miracles you've seen?

Going Deeper

4. How has God prepared you for the hardships you've had to face?

5. What are you praying about or believing in God for right now?

CHAPTER SIX: SCARS

1. How do people treat you?

2. How do you expect to be treated?

3. What do you find yourself doing to keep others from rejecting you?

Going Deeper

4. What do you require of yourself that God does not expect?

5. How do you view your scars?

Chapter Seven: Victim versus Overcomer

1. Are there negative behaviors you have excused in yourself because of the hard things you've gone through?

2. Are there negative behaviors you excuse in those you love because of what they've gone through?

3. How is the pain of your past affecting your present-day life?

Going Deeper

4. Are there ways you are trying to compensate for your loss or trying to prove your value?

5. Can you see your incredible worth aside from your gifts, talents, abilities, and looks?

Chapter Eight: Facing Fears

1. What is your biggest fear?

2. What things would you do if fear wasn't an issue?

3. What role does your comfort zone play in holding you back from experiencing a full life?

Going Deeper

4. What would happen if you chose to be vulnerable?

5. Are you able to confess your sins to others (trust-worthy, safe people)?

CHAPTER NINE: LIES & TRUTHS

1. What lies do you believe that keep your fear in place?

2. What do you think you need to do to be loved and accepted?

3. What would (or do) healthy boundaries look like for you?

Going Deeper

4. What truths in God's words about you are more challenging to believe than lies?

5. Are you making your decisions based on what God says about you or lies you believe about yourself?

CHAPTER TEN: ACCEPTANCE

1. Who are you? What things identify you?

2. What are the most difficult things for you to accept about yourself?

3. Who are you comparing your life to?

Going Deeper

4. What are your strengths? What do you love about yourself?

5. What is the hardest thing for you to forgive yourself for?

CHAPTER ELEVEN: THE WORK OF SUFFERING

1. What has your suffering taught you?

2. What pain are you avoiding?

3. Where is Jesus in your trial?

Going Deeper

4. Have you experienced unforgiveness, bitterness, or hatred as a result of your suffering?

5. Can you trust Jesus with your pain?

CHAPTER TWELVE: WHAT IS IT TO THRIVE?

1. What does thriving mean to you?

2. What areas of life do you need to be more intentional about?

3. What are you thankful for?

Going Deeper

4. What gets in the way of your gratitude?

5. What does God's love for you look like?

Chapter Thirteen: Hope & Wholeness

1. What do you treasure the most?

2. What gifts do you have to share?

3. What things fill you up and give you joy and lasting peace?

Going Deeper

4. What do you hope for?

5. What is your next step from here?

ACKNOWLEDGMENTS

When I consider how richly blessed I am, I think of the amazing people God has added to my life. The people in my life are the cream of the crop. They are faithful, wise overcomers who have taught me so much. I've genuinely been able to experience the love of God through people who have prayed for me, called me at the right time, encouraged me along the way, spoken the truth to me—even when it was hard—and loved me without condition. Honestly, there are too many to name.

Thank you to all.

My family especially—they have been steadfast and constant; they have shaped, influenced, supported, loved, and cared for me every step of the way.

The first responders and the medical team who have risked, sacrificed, and dedicated their lives to helping injured and sick individuals so that they may have the best chance at living a productive and meaningful life.

Daniel and Judy Craft, David and Kathleen Tabor, Dave and Brenda Roever—you are the leaders who have taught me about ministry through your example. You opened my eyes to the truth about myself—even when it wasn't pretty—and the truth about God and His immeasurable grace. I've learned more from you and your courage and humility than I can begin to express. Thank you for seeing me, believing in me, and investing in me.

All my friends, both past and present, who have contributed to my growth and insight. You have helped me live my life to the fullest, taught me through example, brought joy and laughter to my life, cheered me on, listened to my good and bad days, and trusted me. My heart overflows. I'm grateful for all the lessons I've learned from each of you, both the bitter and the sweet. They hold incredible value.

For those of you who have read this book over and over, offering your insight, edits, time, energy, and skill sets, "thank you" is not enough.

This book has been a long project, something that has been on my heart for at least ten years. For me, it's an offering, a gift to God to use as He wishes. Each of you has helped to make this gift a reality. I pray He will "...do superabundantly, far over and above all that we [dare] ask or think [infinitely beyond our highest prayers, desires, thoughts, hopes or dreams] (Ephesians 3:20 AMP)" in your lives.

ABOUT THE AUTHOR

Charity Freeland has a passion for helping hurting people. As one who experienced life-changing tragedy and found freedom and wholeness, she recognizes God has gifted her with hope, insights, and perspectives, not just for herself but to share. Miraculously surviving a disfiguring burn injury at the age of seventeen, God has given her a voice to teenagers, young adults, women, and wounded veterans.

She has spent her career serving various ministries focused on helping youth, crisis survivors, and wounded veterans. She has been able to share her inspiration and wisdom at discipleship training conferences, commencement ceremonies, and churches worldwide.

Charity attended the Phoenix Society's annual "World Burn Congress" multiple times, where she connected with many in the burn community. The Phoenix Society is affecting positive change and providing resources to those who have experienced a burn injury.

Now living in Western Colorado, she enjoys spending time with friends and traveling to see family. She continues to assist and encourage to those with whom she comes in contact.

Made in the USA
Columbia, SC
01 October 2021

46060021R00139